A Cowboy W
in New Mexico

John Sinclair.
© Cynthia Farah, 1988.

A
Cowboy
Writer
in New Mexico

The Memoirs
of
John L. Sinclair

University of New Mexico Press   Albuquerque

Library of Congress Cataloging-in-Publication Data
Sinclair, John L., 1902–
A cowboy writer in New Mexico: the memoirs of John L. Sinclair.
p.   cm.
Includes bibliographical references and index.
ISBN 0-8263-1728-6
1. Sinclair, John L., 1902–   —Biography.
2. Authors—American—20th century—Biography.
3. Museum curators—West (U.S.)—Biography.
4. Cowboys—West (U.S.)—Biography.
I. Title.
PS3537.I846Z466   1966
813'.52—dc20
[B]
92-16120
CIP

All illustrations from the Center for Southwest Research,
General Library, University of New Mexico.

Contents

Preface

John L. Sinclair was a wonderful man and a wonderful story-teller. To John and to hear or read his stories was to want to know him better and to want to hear and to read more of those stories—to wonder along with him, as was his way.

I met John in 1985, when he was eighty-three years old. He was living simply with his wife, Evelyn, and their dogs and cat in a one-room stone cabin with two chimneys on the Santa Ana Pueblo near Bernalillo, New Mexico.

John's health was failing. His eyesight was going from bad to worse, and his legs weren't "working right" any more. He was spending much less time composing on his old portable Royal typewriter and much more time just quietly cogitating in his "new-fangled" wheelchair.

John became my wonderful friend. Later, I became his literary agent, then the publisher of his last novel, *The Night the Bear Came off the Mountain* (The Rydal Press, 1991), and ultimately, and sadly, the executor for his wife's estate and his.

I hadn't known John long or read or listened to many of his stories before I knew I wanted to know him better and to hear and read more of his stories. I especially wondered about his own life story and knew others did too. So in 1988 we conceived a plan. John would tell his story aloud. It would be tape recorded, transcribed, and edited—a long, difficult process that was undertaken by one good friend and eventually completed by another to whom we are all grateful for this book.

The manuscript was finished in 1991. But the health of the Sinclairs was failing. Evelyn fell ill and was hospitalized. Then she was moved into a nursing home. She died in the fall of 1993. A little over a month later, John followed her. He was ninety-one years old. Although I wish this memoir had been published during his lifetime, to read it now is to be in John's company once again and to hear his voice tell his own story at last. *Hasta la vista, amigo!*

Clark Kimball

Santa Fe, New Mexico
October 1995

Foreword

I first met John Sinclair about fifty years ago when he came to the White Lakes area as a ranch hand with the Batercell Cattle Company. He was dipping sheep and cattle, and doing other odd jobs that fall to the hands on a ranch. John and I hit it off right away and became lifelong friends. We never ran out of things to talk about because he was one of the most interesting men that I have had the privilege to call my friend and colleague. John authored one of the best articles ever written about my political career almost twenty-five years ago for *The New Mexico Magazine.*

John married a lovely lady by the name of Evelyn Fox. After John and Evelyn moved to Bernalillo, New Mexico, Evelyn and my mother became fast friends. My mother was a friend to everyone for miles around Stanley. She always had coffee on the stove and something good to eat. People would go for miles to visit my mother to share news, ask her advice and share one of her great home-cooked meals.. Evelyn would ride the bus to our ranch occasionally and stay a week or so, and then John would drive out to the ranch and take her home to Bernalillo.

Over the years, John and I had many conversations about his life, how he came to New Mexico from Scotland and his early days as a ranch hand working on various ranches all across New Mexico from Roswell to Santa Fe. He told me that it was while riding horseback around New Mexico that he fell in love with the state's unique beauty and culture and decided to write about the people and this place called New Mexico. He loved the magnificence and color of New Mexico sunsets, the clear blue skies of autumn, our warm and friendly people and all the things that make New Mexico the Land of Enchantment.

John captured the beauty and essence of New Mexico through his books, articles and stories. His writings are some of the very best works about our people, our culture and our history. He wrote about New Mexico from the inside, as a New Mexican, with an in-depth understanding of the complexity of our multi-cultural society—its heritage and history—with a great sense of humor and with love and respect.

I know you will enjoy *A Cowboy Writer in New Mexico*. It takes me back to the rural days in New Mexico when there were few paved roads and the best transportation to some parts of New Mexico was by horse-back or on foot. New Mexico was one of the last frontiers in America. I am fortunate to have grown to young manhood during the time New Mexico was still a rural state and I am proud to have shared part of its past with my lifelong friend, a truly great New Mexican and outstanding author—John Sinclair.

Governor Bruce King

Santa Fe, New Mexico
March 1994

Introduction

John L. Sinclair and his writings need no introduction to those of us who remember the Land of Enchantment as a whistle-stop between civilized New York and Los Angeles—a still open land of sage and sand sparsely dotted with small villages and a few towns with dirt streets when cowboys were working hands hired to herd cows and mend fences instead of playboys decorating the plaza in Santa Fe with their gaudy silk shirts, designer jeans, and lizard-skin boots.

This book by John Sinclair, who worked fourteen years as a cowboy, brings to later arrivals the people, places, tastes, and smells of that time. But it does more than that. It is a moving recollection of his wealthy and aristocratic family in northern Scotland, of his Scottish sea captain father, of his boyhood years in Scotland and England, his years as a young cowboy on the arid plains of southeastern New Mexico, and the writing of his three unique grassroots novels—*In Time of Harvest, Death in the Claimshack*, and *Cousin Drewey and the Holy Twister*. Through this engrossing narrative runs the thread of his love of the land and his love of simple, earthy people, wherever they are.

I first met John about 1950 at the Coronado State Monument near Bernalillo, where he was serving as its curator. He was a big-boned Scot wearing a large, old Stetson, turquoise bolo, denim jacket, and, of course, cowboy boots. His smile was inviting, his grip firm. We hit it off immediately, having much in common. Both of us had been born in the same year, 1902. Both held salaried jobs, myself at Los Alamos, and were writing meanwhile. He took me to have a cup of coffee and to meet his wife, Evelyn, at their small house adjoining the museum.

In the following years, I saw John often. He was putting the monument in fine shape, arranging the museum's artifacts in display cases, taking visitors to the nearby ruins of the prehistoric Kuaua Pueblo, and explaining the meaning of the painted murals in the ancient kiva. Occasionally he built a big fire in front of the portal, around which Indians and visitors alike sat, listening to him talk.

John was well read in history and anthropology. Before coming to Coronado State Monument, he had worked for three and one-half years as a research assistant at the Museum of New Mexico in Santa Fe and then another two and one-half years as curator of the Lincoln County Museum, housed in the historic courthouse from which Billy the Kid had made his famous escape after killing his guards. Yet John was far from being a stodgy academic—he still looked like a cowboy under that old, battered Stetson.

On a summer Sunday, a group of us would have a picnic lunch on a make-do table overlooking the Rio Grande flowing in front of the monument and overlooked by the Sandia Mountains to the east. Every day there were Indians around from nearby Santa Ana and Zia pueblos crowding the museum and the little house. The Zia women loved John and Evelyn, often bringing them beautiful pottery bowls.

John's favorite pueblo, and mine, was Santa Ana, which is on a high bank of the river across from the monument. Years ago, the people had been moved out, because of the danger of flooding, to new homes near Bernalillo. But they still maintained the pueblo, returning to occupy their apartments twice a year: on midsummer Santa Ana Day, July 26, and on Christmas. We went there each year, both times, to watch the gorgeous tribal dances in the sandy plaza.

Our hosts and lifelong friends were Valencio Garcia, a religious leader, and his family. His house was always open to us, providing cool relief from the baking summer heat, or warmth from the freezing cold outside. The meals served to us were traditionally Indian. Homegrown food of every kind covered the long table. We would bring boxes of store-bought groceries to sweeten the larder, always including a pink-iced cake and chocolate cookies for Valencio's old, blind mother.

Evelyn was a slightly built woman about forty years old. When John met her, she was working as a researcher in the Laboratory of Anthropology in Santa Fe. She and John saw each other frequently until Evelyn left to teach art in high schools in various towns in Texas and Illinois. At Champaign, she did research for the dean of the fine arts department at the University of Illinois. During this period, they corresponded,

Evelyn writing one day that she was returning to New Mexico. John met her when she arrived by train in Albuquerque. An Indian friend drove them home to John's small house at the monument. They were married in Santa Fe in 1947, just three years before I met them both.

Evelyn fitted in at once. She loved the Zia Indians and wanted to know the Santa Anas as well. After a while, she continued teaching art in Indian schools like the one in Acomita, just below the cliffs on which perched ancient Acoma Pueblo. Also, she began to paint oil landscapes of her own and was quite accomplished with a brush.

How little we ever know about each other! So it was with John and me. He never talked about himself, and I didn't pry. The few facts he occasionally mentioned raised questions in my mind about a number of apparent contradictions in his life and his many personal idiosyncrasies. Why did his wealthy and aristocratic Scottish family exclude him from its fortune? How did the son of a Scottish sea captain, who had sailed clipper ships around the Horn into the South Pacific, come to punch cows on the arid plains of New Mexico?

He didn't hold to the cowboy ways even after being one for fourteen years. John didn't like to be crowded by people and liked mountains only at a distance. After he had quit working as a full-time cowboy, he rode the chuck line from one ranch to another, working for a few days and then leaving for his log cabin on the north slope of the Capitan Mountains. He rented the cabin and its 160-acre fenced pasture for five dollars a month. For supplies, he rode with his pack horses to Capitan. Back in his cabin, he was never lonesome. There was time to think of the country he wanted to write about.

In him was a wide streak of Thoreau's austerity and simplicity. John didn't smoke and seldom drank—when he did, it was Scotch, of course. He had not known Indians until he came to the Coronado State Monument. Did his immediate empathy with them stem from his recognition of their own love of the land? From their simplistic, earthy ways? Surely John was an unusual, complex character whom no one really knew. A man who seldom joked but who had written three novels that carried his own indelible brand of high humor.

They tell us much about him. The first one he wrote in the early 1940s while working and living in the Lincoln County Museum. Here, at night, hearing the sounds made by Billy the Kid's ghost, John finally wrote of the people he had known so well as a cowboy riding the range. They were of Appalachian-Ozarkian stock, people who had settled in Oklahoma and then straggled into southeastern New Mexico as nesters and homesteaders. John admired them for their courage, honesty, and earthy humor. And in his first novel, *In Time of Harvest*, he portrays their lives through the dirt-poor McClung family.

Ma and Pa McClung and their five bedraggled children put up a one-room shack on the barren plains and plant beans. It is hard work—-uprooting grass and weeds, turning the soil with handmade tools. The backbreaking toil becomes too much for some of the children. Tewp throws down his hoe and runs off to a ranch to become a free-riding cowboy. He is caught helping Scatterwhiskers steal a Hereford cow and is sent to the state prison for five years. Roddy, another son, skips out when he learns he has made a neighbor girl pregnant. He becomes a railroad tramp. And Sudie becomes a prostitute, wandering from town to town, sitting in drab hotel rooms, thinking of the bean field at home. But Pa and Ma persist. The rows of bean plants keep getting longer, and Pa looks at them with pride. "What more can a man want!" And there are always beans on the McClung table, if nothing else—-bean soup, bean salad, beans boiled, fried, baked, and mashed.

There is pathos here, but viewed with compassionate understanding, written with irresistible humor. The characters are sharply drawn; their vernacular so faultlessly rendered it seems unbelievable that a Scottish ear could have been attuned to it.

Estancia Valley, the central New Mexican setting for this classic novel, was, in the 1920s and 1930s, the producing center for our most cherished fruit of the soil, the pinto bean, and *In Time of Harvest* is its literary monument. It was published in 1943, and for its 1971 reissue I wrote the introduction, recounting the novel's instant and country-wide critical acclaim as "mountain music turned prose and put between bean rows," as the *Chicago Tribune* said in its review. At home in Santa Fe, the perceptive Saul Cohen judged it one of the ten best novels about New Mexico.

Some years later, John followed it with two more novels about the same kind of nesters. The second, *Death in the Claimshack* (1947), tolls the bell on a serious scene converted into a jovial gathering. The title of the third novel, *Cousin Drewey and the Holy Twister* (1981), itself warns us it's a tall tale of rollicking humor. What a cast of characters! Cousin Drewey, from the Ouachita (pronounced Washtaw) Mountains of Oklahoma, is visiting his kinfolk until a holy twister, a he-man cyclone, comes to carry him back to the Washtaws. And among his neighbors are Fats Recknagel, a no-good millionaire rancher, the mail-order lawyer, Shyster Sam Hawkins, a baby-kissing sheriff, Old Man Puckerdo Kazort, and a bunch of bootleggers operating out of Blaylock's Funeral Parlor. Anything can happen with such an assortment, and everything does. All are caricatures, if you will, of solemn citizens in our communities today. Neither of these last two novels ranks with *In Time of Harvest*, but all three are integrated in a unified narrative which has the curious quality of the folklore of a little-known people that has never been equaled in fiction.

"I love to write fiction," said John. "I never outline a story in advance. Just give rein to my imagination and let it take me wherever it goes."

But novels seldom make much money. John began to turn out some two hundred short stories and magazine articles on the topics he knew so well: ghost towns, old mines, historic places, interesting people.

A long break interrupted our friendship. I worked in a Hollywood movie studio. Following my own deep interest in Indians, I went to Mexico and Guatemala on a Rockefeller Foundation research grant to study Aztec and Mayan life and religion. Later, I lived among the Hopi Indians in Arizona, doing research for a comprehensive book on their creation myths and their esoteric religious ceremonials. When I finally returned to live in my own home in Taos, I drove down to resume my friendship with John.

In 1962, he retired after serving eighteen years as curator of the Coronado State Monument. For a while, he and Evelyn lived in southern New Mexico near the Mexican border. Constant sand and dust storms blew them back to the spot they had loved so long. Here, they found and rented from the Santa Ana Pueblo a small, one-room house on a dirt road a few miles northwest of the monument. It became the home John still lives in today.

Aye de mi! How quickly the years slide by! Every writer has his ups and downs, and John has had his. He has received the Golden Spur award from the Western Writers of America, two Wrangler awards from the Cowboy Hall of Fame, and the one he values most, an Honorary Life Membership in the Cowboy Hall of Fame. The downs he has experienced have resulted from Evelyn's failing health and his decreased income. My wife and I see them infrequently, but John telephones me regularly. Without a car, they depend upon friends in Bernalillo to bring them mail and supplies. Evelyn no longer teaches and now lives in a nursing home. John hasn't changed much in appearance, but time has taken its toll on his eyesight and legs. Using a wheelchair, he seldom goes out, and reading glasses are always kept at the typewriter. For he is still writing with a creative urge, strong as ever. There is so much to write about in the form of long stories and more novels!

This, then, is a short sketch of John L. Sinclair as I have known him. A myopic view of a grassroots writer of composite character whose life has spanned horizons beyond my reach. His recollections in these following pages bring it into full focus—they answer all the questions about himself that I didn't ask him, in details his readers will find as exciting as any novel.

This is a book to be happily read and long remembered.

Frank Waters

Tucson, Arizona
February 1990

My First Years

I was born in New York City, where my father represented the Bucknall Steamship Company, a British line. A lot of the Bucknall trade was with New York, and my father was Marine Superintendent, or port captain, of all the Bucknall routes into New York, although each Bucknall ship had its own captain for its voyages. His job was a very important one, and his position in New York allowed him to have an office in the Maritime Exchange. The Maritime Exchange was on Manhattan Island. From it developed what was called the Bush Terminal down on the harbor in Brooklyn. The Bush Terminal was a tremendous warehouse that contained all the offices and storage areas of the steamship companies that traded out of New York, and in front of it was a great line of piers for all the ships, which would sail to the most exotic places of the Orient, the Mediterranean, and Africa—Calcutta, Bombay, Cairo, Tangier. These were not luxury liners like those of the Cunard Line that ran back and forth between New York and Southhampton like ferryboats. These were the "real ships—when ships were ships and not tin cans," as the old sailors used to say of the old wooden ships that my father, a former ship commander, had once sailed.

My father's name was John Leslie Sinclair—the same as mine—the "Leslie" coming from the Scottish clan name of my grandmother. My mother, whose maiden name was Gertrude Corbin, was Irish. Her family name in Ireland had been *Coban*, a word derived from the Gaelic name *Cobhan*, which means "people who live in the harbor." When my mother's father came to America from Ireland, he wanted to be so American that he changed his name to Corbin. My father was in his late thirties when he married my mother around the turn of the century, and she was little more than half his age. I was born December 6, 1902.

We lived in Prospect Park West, a very exclusive part of Brooklyn close to the Bush Terminal and facing Prospect Park. It was a beautiful

John Leslie Sinclair, 1902.

place, with stately houses and mansions. I can just remember my earliest days there.

I can't remember going to school in New York. I don't think I did; I guess they didn't have the strict laws they do now. But I seemed to pick up things at an early age. Mother used to get me books to read, and she taught me arithmetic and other essentials.

Gertrude Corbin Sinclair, circa 1904.

What I recall most vividly of my early childhood is being carried down to the ships by my mother—to the Bucknall ships and those of the other lines. I didn't have anything to do with other boys or girls at that time. I just felt a strong bond with the ships docked at the piers. I especially remember the Bucknall boats, which had an insignia of nine diamonds around their funnels.

The author, circa 1906.

They were wonderful, those ships. Sometimes when they would return from voyages to Africa and India, they would bring back lions, tigers, and huge snakes in cages for zoos in St. Louis and other cities. As a child, I was simply fascinated with this. The ships were always crewed by natives, most of them Lascars—Hindus from India. My father, in fact, could speak a little bit of Hindustani. We would sometimes go onto a ship and into the forecastle down below, where the crew was housed. Not on the bridge and the cabins above but the forecastle—that was where the fascination lay for me. The Lascars were true sailors, but they had brought their Indian ways with them onboard. They dressed only in loincloths and turbans. They had goats running around on the decks which they would butcher for meat. They had stores of rice and ginger. And curry—everything they cooked had curry in it. The smells were wonderful.

My father had the sea in his blood, and my mother and I received our love of the sea from him. All we ever heard about was ships. Officers from the Bucknall line and from other British lines would come to visit us in our home when the ships came in, and I remember them all. My mother would get the *New York Times* every day, and she would first turn to the shipping news to see where the ships were going— where they were bound and which ones were coming into New York. She knew that she would soon see some of the officers in our home.

One of those who came to visit us was Captain Linklater of the *Blumfontein*. As a little, tiny kid, I used to sit on his lap and listen to my parents and him talk about ships and ocean voyages, and I drank it all in. Captain Linklater, after a while, went onto another ship called the *Karima*, a Bucknall boat. I learned, much later, when I was in Cambridge, that Captain Linklater had died when his ship was wrecked off the coast of Ceylon. The crew got off the ship, but the captain stayed and went down with it.

That was normal for British captains in those days. It wasn't only sentiment. It was because of what they'd have to go through; they would rather die than face the terrible courts of inquiry. My father would have gone down with his ship if it had sunk while he was captain. The *Loch Vennachar*, the wool clipper that my father had sailed, didn't have any engines; it was all sails. Some of these clippers were so fast and so dependent on their sails that the sails could actually sink the ships when heavy winds got ahold of them. After my father left her, the *Loch Vennachar* eventually did go down, and the captain of the ship, Captain Ozanne, went down with it. I'm sure they don't follow that custom now.

That's the kind of life I lived for my first four years—sheltered but adventurous, surrounded by seamen and tales of ships and seafaring life. Then in 1906, my father died of Bright's disease, from drinking too much, like so many other sea captains. Suddenly, my mother and I were left alone—and her life had been no less sheltered socially than my own. The only people she really knew were officers of British steamships. Knowing she could not raise me the way my father would have wanted, as a Scottish gentleman, she notified my grandfather in Scotland that my father had died and that she was left with me to provide for. It must have been a shock for my grandfather—not only to hear that his son had died, but that he had a daughter-in-law and a grandson. My father had never told him about us.

The Sinclairs

The Sinclairs, my ancestral family in Scotland, were northern Scots, with more Scandinavian blood in them than the Celtic Irish or the Highland Scots had. The clan descended from Norman knights who had come to Scotland in the Middle Ages. By the sixteenth century, they had reached the height of their power in Caithness, on the extreme northeastern tip of the Scottish mainland, and our family descended directly from the chief of the clan.

The Sinclairs had a turbulent history from the beginning of their time in Scotland. There were many bloody clan battles and border feuds, the last one fought in 1680. Then, during the Battle of Culloden, which marked the end of the Jacobite rebellion of 1745, the clan fought alongside the Highlanders to try to restore the Scottish pretender, Charles Edward Stuart, to the throne. The English and the Lowland forces came over and defeated them in the battle, which turned into a great slaughter.

To punish the Highlanders and all who had fought with them, the king of England enacted the proscription of 1746, which banned everything pertaining to Highland life—wearing the kilt, playing the bagpipe, and carrying daggers or guns. They even wanted to take away the Gaelic language. The proscription lasted until 1783, when a succeeding king lifted the ban and allowed the return of the traditional Highland lifestyle.

It was then that my great-great-grandfather, wanting to do something to help restore Scottish traditions, decided to be a manufacturer of tartans. The firm he founded made the septs, the tartan patterns for the Scottish clans, each clan's design unique. With the septs were produced the kilts, leggings, and everything else necessary for this Highland Scottish distinction. The firm, established in Edinburgh, passed eventually to my great-grandfather and then to my grandfather, David Sinclair.

*David Sinclair (my
grandfather), circa 1885.*

In 1860 my grandfather married the woman who was to be my
grandmother. She was a Balgoney Leslie and very aristocratic. Her people
were great landowners in Aberdeenshire, north of Edinburgh. My grandfather would not have married anyone else, of course. The most important thing was the line—carrying on the line. The first child born
of that marriage was my aunt Mary, the second my uncle David, and
the third John, my father, who was born on September 1, 1863.

Under my grandfather's strong hand, the firm he had inherited began to grow. Branching out far beyond its basis in tartans, the firm
established a linen mill in Londonderry in northern Ireland, where it
manufactured Irish linens. To the tartans were added tweeds, and soon
the emphasis was on the more common Scottish textiles. The Sinclairs
were an Edinburgh family, but the firm became so large that the family
began to divide their time between Edinburgh and Glasgow. Then by
the time my father was born, they had moved to Glasgow, although
they kept a residence in Edinburgh.

Elizabeth Leslie (my grandmother), circa 1860.

It was very important that the three children be educated properly, so my father was sent first to Germany for a year and then to France for another. I believe he was around twelve when he went to Europe. When he came back, his father said, "Now we are going to send you to a school in England to get a good British education." The school selected was one of the boarding schools for the upper-class British, and it was at this point that my father began to feel strongly that the family was becoming too anglicized.

About this time, my father's mother died. He had loved her deeply, and losing her seemed to intensify his reaction to the family's slide into anglicization. Then in 1877, my grandfather married for the second time. She was a MacKinnon, a Scottish woman from Glasgow. Although

9

the MacKinnons didn't have the bloodlines that the Sinclairs or Leslies had, she was very well educated—she had good schooling and rearing. But my father didn't get along with his new stepmother, and so when he was about sixteen years old, he ran off to Glasgow, down to the *broomielaw*, or the docks, and signed onto a sailing ship.

They would take anybody on those ships. It was virtually slave labor. His first voyage was to Halifax, Nova Scotia, and he said afterward that he would never forget it. They were physically abusive, kicking him around and treating him almost brutally. When he completed the return voyage from Halifax, he got off the ship at Glasgow with tremendous relief and said to himself that he never wanted to see the ocean again.

When he went to see my grandfather at the family home in Kelvin Grove, up near the University of Glasgow, he told my grandfather, "I am ready to go to England now and go back to school. Do what you want to do with me. Things are different now."

My grandfather shook his head. He said, "No, you've made your bed and you're going to lie in it. I've already made arrangements to have you apprenticed to the P & O Steamship Company." So my father entered the Peninsular and Oriental as a cadet on their ships.

The Peninsular and Oriental was a big steamship company that ran between Britain and India. As a cadet and later a mate, my father would come back to Glasgow once in a while and see his family; then off he would go again on another ship to India, China, and all over the East. Finally, he got to Melbourne, and he decided that this city would be his home port. He didn't particularly want to go back to London to see his father and his stepmother.

While my father was at sea, my grandfather's business had moved its head offices to London, although it kept the warehouses and the mills going in Glasgow and Londonderry. The move was a profitable one because it enabled my grandfather to expand his export business. He had taken on two partners, a Colonel Tilley and a Mr. Henderson, and the firm was now called Tilley and Henderson. This shift also brought with it a great change for the family because it demanded a considerable amount of socializing with the English. This simply rocked the foundations of the family. It was the beginning of ruined family rela-

Mary Sinclair Smith
(my aunt), circa 1885.

tionships, for it heralded the complete anglicization of the purely Scottish Sinclairs.

My grandfather settled on three acres of land on the outskirts of London, living in a mansion named Craig Ard, which means "High Rock." My uncle David, the older son, had stayed with my grandfather all of the time, and now he went into the firm as a partner.

Vida, the child of the second marriage, had pure Scottish blood, but she was born and brought up in England. From the time of her birth, my grandfather, his new wife, my uncle, and this new addition to the family were all together in one house. My aunt Mary, the oldest daughter, was by then married and still lived in Scotland.

As my father worked on different ships, his skill as a mariner grew. I still have the discharge papers from all of his voyages, and there were

Vida Rosalind Sinclair (Aunt Vida), circa 1885.

many. At twenty-five, he was too young to earn his master's certificate, but although he couldn't yet command a ship, he was often able to serve as a mate of some kind; on one voyage he would be third mate, and on another he would be first mate. He made voyages everywhere, particularly later, when he changed from the P & O steamships to the clipper ships. He never sailed on the *Cutty Sark*, the great tea clipper that raced other ships from Calcutta around Cape Horn in order to get to the Thames with the first of the tea harvest and to claim the bounty. But he did sail on the *Loch Vennachar*, a wool clipper out of Melbourne that raced to London with other wool clippers to win the prize.

My father finally got his master's certificate in 1888. That entitled him to command any of the British ships. Now he was a certified mariner, and in 1890 or so he commanded his first ship. He made voyages on all kinds of ships; some had engines with less horsepower than many automobile engines today.

In Melbourne, my father was married, for the first time, to an Australian woman, and there they had two children. Then he was transferred to Calcutta, and he took his wife and two children with him. They had not lived there long, a year maybe, when both children died very young from the terrible diseases that ravaged India during that time. Soon after that, my father decided he would like to go back to Britain and live in London. He would follow the sea, but he would make London his home port.

He took his Australian wife with him. Now, she was not an aristocrat—she was one of those ruddy-faced Australians—but he wanted to present her to my grandfather and settle down nearby. At this point, he had already established a connection in London with the Bucknall Steamship Company, whose trade at that time was not so much with India as with Africa and the Mediterranean countries. The Suez Canal was being used then, and they didn't have to go around Cape Horn to reach India and Australia, but the line still ran to Cape Town and all the South African ports.

The day came when my father took his wife to be presented to his father, his stepmother, and his stepsister. He had notified them that he wanted his wife to meet them, but they had never answered his letter. Nevertheless, my father and his wife hired a carriage and went out to the suburban mansion where Grandfather lived. My father brought his wife to the door, and when the butler opened it, they introduced themselves. The butler said simply, "I have instructions that Mr. Sinclair will not receive you," and backed off and closed the door—bang. In shock, they turned around and went back downtown, and soon afterward Father's first wife just wasted away and died of a broken heart. She had been rejected because she wasn't of the same social class as the Sinclair family.

My father swore then that he was going to get out of London and away from those people as quickly as he possibly could. He was soon offered an executive position as port captain of the Bucknall Steamship Company in New York, and he accepted it; his days on the vessels were over. He vowed that if he ever married again, he would never tell his family back in London, and that's just what he did.

London, 1912

After my mother told my grandfather about Father's death and about my existence, we lived for a few years with her sister, Marguerite. Mother continued to get the *New York Times* every day to read the shipping news and see where the steamers were all over the world. And officers from the Bucknall boats used to come over and visit her; for a time, I thought she might marry one of them, a Mr. Baker of the *Kansas*, but she never remarried.

By 1912, when I was ten years old, my future was finally decided. I was told that I was being sent to Britain so that my grandfather could adopt me and ensure continuance of the pure Sinclair line. My uncle David had never remarried, and so I was the only hope to carry on the lineage. If I were to be brought up properly, it would have to happen in England.

I didn't like the idea; I didn't want to leave my mother. But my mother and my aunt took me down to the dock anyway—to the *St. Paul*. It was an American ship, and the captain had been a friend of my father's; all those sea captains and engineers and officers knew each other. Mother introduced me to him, and asked him to keep his eye on me during the voyage because otherwise I'd be all alone. I remember how I stood on the ship as it was pulling out. It pulled out very, very slowly. My mother walked down to end of the pier as we pulled away, and I could see her standing there, waving to me. I waved back, and that was the last time I saw her.

Mother died only three years later. Grief from losing me is probably what caused her death. First her beloved husband and then her little son. It just broke her heart.

The *St. Paul* left New York bound for Liverpool, and the crossing took about six days. It was a slow crossing, but I had fun with the other boys on the ship. I remember they had a big shipment of silver—big

My uncle, David Sinclair (left), and my father, John Sinclair, 1888.

Captain John Sinclair, circa 1888.

blocks of solid silver—that was being shipped from America to England. The blocks were being moved from one section of the deck to another, and all of us boys were given a kind of hoe and were told to help the men slide those blocks of silver along the deck like shuffleboard disks. Then a sailor would pick them up, and they would go into a hopper. That's all I can remember of that voyage.

I do remember that when the ship entered the Mersey River, it stopped for a time before going into the dock at Liverpool. And I had no idea how I was going to be met or anything. I just didn't know and

I was terrified—absolutely terrified. When the ship at last pulled into the dock, I must have waited there for two or three hours. I thought to myself, "Now, where do I go from here?" I didn't know anyone in Liverpool. Finally, a man came up to me. He was from Thomas Cooke, a touring agency that had offices all over the world. My uncle and my grandfather had instructed him to meet the ship and take me down to the Lime Street Station in Liverpool to catch a train to London.

They did not come there to meet me! They hired someone to put me on that train! I was ten years old, in a foreign country, and I was put on a train all by myself to go to London.

I had no idea who would meet me in London either. I thought, "Well, surely it will be my grandfather or my uncle who will meet me in Euston Station when the train gets in." But nobody was there when I got off. I had a trunk in the luggage car, and someone took it off and put it in the baggage room. And I just waited there all alone. Eventually this man came up to me and said, "I'm from Thomas Cooke, and I'm going to take you over to the house where your people are." So we got into a cab, and we drove over to Palace Court—Number 14, Palace Court.

The man took me up to the door of my grandfather's house and rang the bell. My grandfather and Aunt Vida had gone to bed, and so had all the servants. It was late, very late—it must have been about eleven or twelve o'clock. Only my uncle David had stayed up, and it was he who came to the door.

As the firstborn son of my grandfather, it was Uncle David, and not my father, who should have been the one to pass on the Sinclair line; but my uncle had never married, and so now the responsibility had fallen to the ten-year-old boy standing in the doorway—myself.

My uncle took me into his study, where he had been reading while waiting for me to arrive. He asked me a lot of questions about the voyage and about the train ride from Liverpool to London. He told me they were going to put me in school—was I anxious to go to school? Of course, I was; I felt so alone then that I would have done anything they told me to do. We talked for a little while longer, and then he said, "Well, I'll show you up to your bedroom." He never asked me about my mother.

17

The next morning, before I was up, he and my grandfather went off to their offices. Cowell, the chauffeur, had come by very early and picked them up in the Rolls-Royce. The first person I met in the daylight was Aunt Vida; I breakfasted with her that morning, as I did from then on.

Aunt Vida was in her early thirties and spoke with a very upper-class British accent, with such broad *a*'s and *r*'s that she sounded like she had adenoids. At later breakfasts, she would always give me a lesson in our ancestry, and on one occasion—I will never forget this—she told me, "You were born in a pigsty, but that doesn't mean to say you are a pig." Fortunately, on this first morning with her, she didn't ask me too many questions, but she did tell me what a wonderful life I was going to have. She said I would become a real Englishman.

It was easy to understand why my father had developed such a dislike of Aunt Vida, his stepsister. In photographs of her from childhood, you could see that she was spoiled to the point of wickedness; you could tell by the look on her face.

Uncle David was easier to get along with, but he was under the sway of Vida—how much so I would find out later, when Grandfather died and they were designated trustees of the estate.

That first day I also met my stepgrandmother, who seemed very nice and almost always treated me well—except for occasionally saying things about Americans and my mother that hurt me. Otherwise, we got along very well.

I didn't meet my grandfather, a big man with a thick Scottish burr, until it was time to have dinner that night. Of course, during the day, he and my uncle had gone over to one of the clubs. They were both members of the Carlton Club. No one belonged to it unless they were of the highest aristocracy or prominent in government. I saw the club later. There were a lot of easy chairs to sit in, newspapers and magazines to read, and a dining room. Grandfather and Uncle David always had lunch at the club, which in those days was strictly for men. I think Margaret Thatcher is a member of the Carlton Club now.

My uncle also belonged to the Bath Club. One day he asked me to meet him there, and when I came in I saw him talking to three men. I knew better than to interrupt, so I sat and waited for them to finish.

The author, circa 1910.

When the men left, my uncle came over to me and told me who they were. One was the Prince of Wales, the future king of England, who later abdicated the throne.

I came to love my grandfather very much. When I was away at school, I would sometimes go to London on holidays, and my grand-father and I would go out for walks nearby at Kensington Gardens, where Kensington Castle is located. It had elaborate flower gardens, and a pond where small boys sailed model boats. As my grandfather and I talked, he explained many things to me about the family and their business.

Craig Ard, my grandfather's former residence in London, had been quite an estate. There were stables there, where he kept Cleveland Bay horses for the carriage that had taken him and my uncle down to their offices in the heart of the city. The horses were beautiful—I've seen pictures—but to my grandfather they were only a means of transportation, nothing more. They also had polo ponies—small thoroughbreds.

Then they moved from Craig Ard further into London, into the Bayswater District, and they got the house there at Number 14 Palace Court, a very exclusive street. It was then that they got a car, the Rolls-Royce. Cowell, who had taken care of the horses and the coach at Craig Ard, now became the chauffeur of the Rolls-Royce at Palace Court. My grandfather and uncle would eat breakfast early—they were finished by eight o'clock in the morning—and then put on their top hats and sit in the Rolls-Royce while Cowell drove them to their offices on Silver Street.

Grandfather also had a second home, a lodge called Dalreoch in the Scottish Highlands, not far from the little village of Enoch Dhu. This wasn't a log cabin; it was practically a mansion. Mrs. Souter was the housekeeper, and there were also two or three maids there to keep the lodge going. My uncle and grandfather went to all that expense for maybe one month of stag and grouse hunting every year.

The way we lived at Palace Court didn't impress me favorably. I was not impressed by elegance, and hated the formality of life there.

Dinner was an ordeal. A servant would come to the hall and sound a gong to announce that dinner would be served in about an hour. We were then expected to take a bath and dress for dinner—you couldn't eat without dressing. We had to have slippers on because the floor was highly polished and would be scuffed by shoes, and the men had to wear dress trousers, a dinner jacket, and a tie. Then we'd all go into the dining room, sit in the same old place at the table, and have plates placed before us. The napkins were always wrapped up in rings, and it was a glass for this and a glass for that, and one fork for the main course and another for the fish, and so forth—and then there would always be

No. 14 Palace Court. My room was located on the second story, left. The servants' quarters are seen at the right rear.

one spoon for the soup and another for the dessert. We'd sit down, with my grandfather over at the head of the table, and then the maids would start serving, always from the left; they'd hold a dish for you, and you'd put a little bit on your plate. Oh, the manners! I was always being told that I'd done this or that wrong.

One consolation was that only choice foods were served at Palace Court. We'd have a soup first—vegetable soup or consommé—and then a fish course, sole maybe, with delicious sauce. For the main course, we'd often have roast beef and potatoes. The roast beef of England was wonderful, with a lot of fat on it that made it flavorful; nowadays, we have the fat taken off, and the flavor's gone. For the vegetable course, we might have cauliflower áu gratin. Following that we'd have the dessert—puddings of different kinds or pastries, and then we were always expected to retire to the library upstairs for the demitasse, a very, very small cup of terribly strong coffee, almost like syrup.

The food was good, but it was very hard to enjoy dinner because you had to be so precise about eating it.

There were eight servants at Palace Court, including Cowell, the chauffeur. There was Dober, the butler; Mr. Taylor, the cook; Katherine, who was retired but had been allowed to live on with the servants at Palace Court because she had been my aunt Vida's nanny. Then there were Mary and Edie; Mary was the serving maid in the dining room, and Edie was a scullery maid who washed the dishes, silverware, and pots and pans. There were eight in all, and all were kept busy.

Leading to the stairway to the second floor was a stairway carpeted with a beautiful blue carpet all the way up. There was a banister on one side of the stairway, and on the other side a wall on which paintings of our ancestors were hung. This beautiful blue carpet had rods below each step to hold it down, and many times I'd go up the stairs, and there would be a servant girl polishing the rods, getting them to shine. I felt so sorry for her; it seemed almost like slavery. One day I stopped to talk with her. She didn't say much, but I talked with her anyway for a while. My uncle saw us, and when I came down the stairs he called me into his study and bawled me out. I was not to talk to the servants; they were lower class.

Schooling in Britain

My grandfather, uncle, and aunt were committed to removing everything American from me and replacing it with upper-class English. The first part of their campaign was to almost immediately send me to public school in England—to Beacon, in Crowborough, Sussex County, on the south coast. In Britain, a public school is very, very private, open only to the aristocracy and the wealthy; they darned sure aren't open to the public. As a Sinclair, of course, I qualified.

I lasted two years at Beacon. While there I took the usual studies—reading, writing, arithmetic—and always French. At public schools in Britain, they start you with French when you're very, very young, and then you move into Latin and, eventually, to Greek.

I was miserable at Beacon, living among a bunch of aristocratic English schoolboys who couldn't have been more foreign to me. As young as I was, I'd already developed an animosity toward the English people and to English life, and particularly to the upper class, the only English class I knew, or was permitted to know.

I didn't see much of the family during my school years in Britain because in the Scottish aristocracy parents saw very little of their children. Each new child was given immediately to a nanny. When too old for a nanny, he or she was sent abroad to go to school or down to England, away from the family. Then on holidays, the family would be together for a little while; and then the children would be sent somewhere else, perhaps to the seashore. The children only became a part of the family when they turned twenty-one.

It was while on such holidays that I came to know and love my aunt Mary and her family, who lived in Helensburgh in the Highlands of Scotland. Like my father, Aunt Mary was very bitter toward my grandfather because of the second marriage, and like me, she took great pride in our Scottish descent.

Aunt Mary had married Frank Smith, who was in the pig-iron business. Their last name is not the same "Smith" as the one so common in America; Smith is the name of a very distinct clan in Scotland, related, I think, to the MacEwens and other Highland clans.

Aunt Mary and Uncle Frank had several homes, including one in London at 65 Wellington Road, with housekeepers at each one; but Aunt Mary would visit each house only two or three weeks a year, always returning to their Highlands home. She would never leave Scotland.

I felt my roots were in Scotland also.

My family, seeing I was unhappy at Beacon, decided to pull me out of school. My grandfather seemed interested then in having me follow in my father's footsteps, and so I was sent to Osborne, the naval academy on the south coast of England. I would probably be in the navy a couple of years, and then I could join the Merchant Marines. I was willing to go to the academy, but, unlike my family, I wasn't interested in all the pomp and ceremony that went with the navy; I would much rather have simply hired onto a rusty old ship like the ones my father had sailed. After an eye examination, however, it was determined that my vision wasn't good enough to continue with a naval career. What then was to be done with me?

The family had already decided that they didn't want me to follow in the textile business; my uncle had that cinched. At that time—this was during World War I—my grandfather's company had both cotton mills and woolen mills in Scotland. My grandfather and uncle were prospering. They were making regular trips to Australia to buy wool and bringing the wool by ships to the mills in Scotland.

They were also sending for cotton from America. The United States government had to clothe their troops stationed in England, so they had contracted with Tilley and Henderson, my grandfather's firm, to weave military shirts for the soldiers. The shirts were made out of cotton that Tilley and Henderson ordered from Sea Island, Georgia, where they grew the finest cotton available; the family would deal with American firms if they could get a profit out of it—even if, all the while, they hated America and Americans.

The linen mill in Londonderry was also doing fine, although it had become completely anglicized and no longer produced the Scottish tartans and tweeds, but primarily cottons and linens.

Then the Londonderry linen mill was blown up by the Sinn Fein, a political division of the Irish Republican Army. It was the southern Irish, from the area my mother's people had come from, who bombed the mill. So now the family had an animosity toward the Irish, especially toward my mother's family.

Since both the navy and the textile business were closed to me, it was decided to send me back to public school; then when I turned seventeen, I would take the eye examination for the navy again, and maybe I would pass this time. So I was sent to Perse School, in Cambridge—a very old and very exclusive school founded by Dr. Stephen Perse in the late 1500s.

Perse was a prep school for the university and went up to the sixth form, the equivalent of the second year in an American university. After the sixth form, there were two other forms for those who wanted to enter the university—the special sixth to prepare you for university course work and the classical sixth in which you learned ancient Greek in order to take the Cambridge entrance examination.

The entrance examination for Cambridge was called the tripos—Greek for "three-legged," for the three-legged stool the examiner would sit on while grilling you. The examiner, also called a tripos, was a Cambridge don, and he would put on a little peaked cap, sit on his high, three-legged stool, and ask questions in ancient Greek that you had to answer in ancient Greek.

My grandfather and uncle decided that I would study for this examination, and I did study Greek, in the fifth and sixth forms. But I never completed the classical sixth, and I never took the tripos. I despised academics and had no desire to go on to Cambridge. In fact, one of the schoolmasters characterized me as a weak student, my only talent appearing to be poetry and writing. He was right. I certainly wasn't a scholar, and I didn't want to be one. I can't remember any Greek at all today.

Latin was another language I never mastered. For a while, I remember, we had to talk Latin at breakfast, asking in Latin for the bread to be passed and for the "Spotted Dog." Spotted Dog is a pudding of suet and raisins—just awful! It was bad enough to have to eat it in English, but to have to eat it in Latin was asking too much.

There were several Scottish students at Perse, but most of my classmates were horrible. They were all gentlemen's sons, and just nasty—to me anyway. I wasn't used to that, and I didn't like them at all. Even so, some of the students were rather interesting. World War I was going on while I was at Perse, and because of the turmoil in Europe, there were a lot of Serbians at the school, some of them members of the royal family, the Karageorgeviches.

Gaekwad was another student. He was the heir to the Gaekwar of Boroda, one of the richest rajahs of India. The Gaekwar, Gaekwad's uncle, was famous because when Edward VII had the durbar—when all the rajahs of India were supposed to go up before the king of England and then back out, never turning their back on the king—the Gaekwar of Boroda walked up there, stood before the king, and turned his back on him and walked out. He was made famous for that.

Gaekwad, my fellow student, went on to the university—to Trinity—and later succeeded his uncle as the Gaekwar of Boroda. But by then, I think the British had put all the rajahs under a pension, and they didn't have the same power they once had. When that happened, Gaekwad traveled to California and hung around Hollywood; then he went down to Florida and finally died. He was something of a playboy.

Another notable person at Perse was the headmaster, Dr. H. D. Rouse, who was later famous for translating *The Odyssey* and *The Iliad*. I didn't like Dr. Rouse's classes very much, but I liked him; he was a very nice person. He was a short, dumpy man and raised hogs in the back of the boarding house on Glebe Road, which was way out in the country. He raised the pork that we used to eat in school.

War, of course, was always in the air while I was at Perse School, and I was in the Officer Training Corps. In 1916, we were digging trenches out on the Gogmagog Hills for British troops to make a stand if the Germans invaded England—and we expected they might. My cousin, Leslie Smith, my aunt Mary's only son, was killed in that war. He'd been injured and later died of the injuries. He'd been in the Royal Garrison Artillery.

I remember the day the war ended: November 11, 1918. There was a bus that made a regular stop by our boardinghouse, going to and from town. That day, we jumped onto that bus without paying any money—we didn't care to pay anything, and they wouldn't have taken it if we had offered it to them. We rode down into Cambridge, and everybody was running around in the streets celebrating. It was terrific.

It was also while I was at Perse, during my last year there, early in 1919, that I was told my grandfather had died. He was eighty-one years old. I would miss him very much.

After Grandfather's death, the family asked me what I would like to do when I finished school, and I said that I would like to be a farmer, that I had a keen interest in the land and wanted to breed livestock, especially sheep. I had read quite a bit on farming and livestock by then and was very interested in the subject. In fact, at Perse School, I had subscribed to a tabloid magazine, *The Farmer and Stock Breeder*, and liked the idea of getting into something like that. So the family decided that I would first undergo an apprenticeship, and then go to the colonies, where I could establish a farming or a livestock operation for the family.

I was told I could choose Canada, Australia, or New Zealand; but I knew they weren't particularly interested in having me go to Australia—my uncle already had a vested interest there, and he didn't want me to have any part of it. On one of their voyages to Australia to buy wool, my grandfather and uncle ended up in the western part, not far from Perth, where there was a parcel of land for sale. The land—one hundred square miles of it—was thick with a valuable timber called jarrah. This wood is highly resistant to termites, and in those days it was in great demand in the British colonies for railway ties. So they bought the hundred square miles and started to market the timber, intending to put livestock on the land once it was cleared.

In 1919, after I completed my studies at Perse, I was apprenticed to the estate of the Duke of Buccleuch at Drumlanrig Castle in Dumfriesshire, Scotland. My father's cousin, Dr. Hewitt, made all the arrangements. He was a minister in the town of Rothessay on the Island of Bute off the coast of Scotland, and well acquainted with the Buccleuch family. It was decided that after my apprenticeship I would go to British Columbia in western Canada to establish a farming operation there.

The author, circa 1919.

Apprenticeship in Scotland

When I started at the duke's estate, my wages were nine shillings a week, or about two dollars and fifty cents a week in American currency. That was all right—I was learning; I was being apprenticed. And my uncle paid for my board.

The work on the farms was hard work, but it was very enjoyable. On Sundays—the only days for relaxation—I might visit the neighboring farms or go off to see my aunt Mary and her family in the western part of Scotland. I visited them quite often; that was my second home. I would take the train to Glasgow from Carronbridge Station in Thornhill, the village near the castle. Then I'd change stations in Glasgow and take the West Highland Railway to Helensburgh, down in the Firth of Clyde, from Glasgow. I always enjoyed visiting them.

The duke's estate was so large that twenty-five miles of the Glasgow and Southwestern Railway ran across it, and on it there were several farms. I spent the first year and a half of my apprenticeship at Drumlanrig Gardens learning about the growing of fruit. The family wanted me to grow Jonathan apples in British Columbia. They didn't have the Jonathan apple in Scotland, but I worked with Gloucester Pearmain, Bramley's Seedling, and other British varieties.

At Drumlanrig Gardens, there were about five acres of greenhouses. They also had large outdoor plots for the growing of vegetables. But very few of the tree fruits as we know them here in the United States could be grown out-of-doors there; the climate was just too raw. Plums and all kinds of berries could be grown out-of-doors, but the Bramley Seedling, a sour, green cooking apple, was the only apple that would survive the climate there. So a lot of the fruit trees had to be grown in greenhouses.

There was one greenhouse that ran the entire length of the five acres. In fact, down the middle of that greenhouse was a railway, and a truck ran on the rails from one end to the other. It was a moving platform, and from that platform we could tend the fruit trees, which were trained using wires. A peach tree would grow and be spread out like a fan, with the fruit hanging on it. We would disbud the tree so that there would only be a few peaches on each little shoot. The peaches grew to an enormous size and were very, very delicious.

Outside, the greenhouses were surrounded by brick walls. Along these walls grew Victoria plum trees, which were nailed and trained in fan shapes against the walls. We had a whole row of plum trees covering the length of the five acres. On some of the walls they had what they called cordons. A cordon was a tree—usually an apple—that had one stem or trunk trained from top to bottom against the wall with nails. Pruning had to be done, of course, to train the cordon. There was always plenty of fruit on cordoned trees.

Tomatoes were also grown in the greenhouses; they were fabulous and in absolute abundance. In the field, we would grow turnips to feed the cattle. They were delicious, and everyone would eat them. They would grow to be twenty pounds apiece.

Fruits and vegetables grew to enormous size in Scotland, both outdoors and in the greenhouses. Scotland being so far north, the days are very long during the growing season, and anything planted over there grows. There were days when the sun would come up about two A.M. and go down about ten P.M. Between these two times there was continuous daylight—a sort of twilight—which, particularly at the end of June, was called the *simmer glim* (summer gleam).

One of my jobs was to select fruit and put it in boxes filled with sphagnum moss. I'd select a choice peach and put it in the box, then three others to make a row; and then I'd make two more rows and one more layer on top. There'd be maybe two dozen peaches per box. There was a boy there with a cart that was pulled by a donkey, and he would take these boxes in his cart down to the railroad station to be shipped to fruit wholesale houses. Drumlanrig Gardens was a commercial business. All of the produce was grown strictly for sale and was shipped to Glasgow.

One of the head gardeners at Drumlanrig Gardens was named John Arthur Thomson—this was before my time, in the late 1800s—and

A view of Drumlanrig Castle, home of the Duke of Buccleuch, from the gardens. The stream is called Marr Burn.

while he was there, Thomson carried out some significant experiments in grape growing. He had a special greenhouse where he was trying to develop a seedless grape. Then he moved on to his own place in Galashiels, in another part of Scotland, and opened his own nursery. There he continued his work and finally succeeded in creating the Thomson Seedless Grape, for which he was knighted.

A man named Stuart eventually took his place at the gardens. Stuart had been the head gardener to the nobility at Lauderdale, a very famous place on the Scottish border. Before that, he was head gardener at the royal family's castle, Glamis, which Shakespeare made famous in *Macbeth* and where the queen mother was born.

After I had been at Drumlanrig Gardens about a year, horticulture kind of lost its excitement for me, although I still wanted to go to British Columbia and have an orchard and a fruit farm there. But I also wanted a cattle ranch, and so I wanted to learn cattle and sheep raising on one of the duke's other farms.

Scotland is supreme in the raising of beef cattle. The finest cattle in the world are there—the Aberdeen Angus, the Shorthorn, and the Galloway. The duke's estate was in an area of southern Scotland where the valleys, or glens, are very lush and green, in places rich in timber and elsewhere highly cultivated. When you move out of the glens or valleys, the hills are covered with heather. All of it is prime grazing land—sheep and cattle country and the world of the Border collie.

In Scotland, farms were considered landmarks, so their names were very important, and farmers were often even called after the names of their farms. On the duke's estate there was a farm called Tibbers, which got its name from a castle built by the Romans along the Tibbers River in Julius Caesar's time. The ruins were still there on a hill above a field where we grew ryegrass for hay—the same field in which Julius Caesar's soldiers grew hay for their horses.

Tibbers was the home farm of the duke, and it was famous for the breeding of Shorthorn and Galloway cattle. The Galloway are a very small, black breed, longhaired and relatively hornless. From them was developed the Angus, which is larger and smooth and hornless; but we had no Angus at Tibbers. The duke's registered Galloways and Shorthorns were in great demand because of their high pedigree, and they were sent all over the world.

At Tibbers, the cattle were raised in the usual Scottish fashion of letting them graze out-of-doors for most of the year, except for extreme winter, when they were brought into the byres. The byres were long, long stone sheds where the cattle were chained up to feed troughs. Dairy cattle stayed in them all winter, kept warm by their own body heat. From the cold, bleak Scottish winter day or night, you could go into the byre, and it would be just as warm as if it were heated by a furnace.

After Tibbers, I worked for about a year at another farm on the estate called The Drum. *Drum* is a Gaelic word meaning "hill," and this farm was, indeed, on a hill. There I learned all the families of Shorthorn—the Queen Anne, the Cherry Blossom, and others—all the way back to the beginning of the breed. The duke was also celebrated for breeding what was called the Blue-Grey, which was the result of the mating of a white Shorthorn bull with a black Galloway cow. It didn't set a breed, yet generally, when a calf was born, it was sort of a bluish-white color, longhaired like the Galloway, and hornless. It was a beautiful calf and the choicest beef that could be had anywhere in the world. The Blue-Greys were shipped on trains to Smithfield Market in London.

While I was at The Drum, I also took an interest in the Ayershire, a dairy breed. Ayershires were all pedigreed—all had names—and the bulls were celebrated among the farmers of that area like star football players are today in Dallas or Denver. These wonderful, beautiful cattle were famous for their milk, which was the finest for making cheese and other dairy foods. They were also a very tough breed. The climate was so terrible that a Jersey, Guernsey, or Hereford would succumb to tuberculosis; they were accustomed to the warmth of southern England. But the Ayershire thrived in Scotland.

I was fascinated with the feeding and selection of the breeding stock of these marvelous cattle. I fed the Ayreshires turnips in the byre in the winter, and I took them out to the pasture in the summer. I got up at three in the morning, jumped on my bicycle, and rode the six miles from where I stayed to milk the cows at The Drum. There were about sixty I had to milk, and, of course, we had a milking machine. It ran on petrol. In the winter, the milk—which was very sweet—was taken down to the railway station and shipped into Glasgow. There the big dairies would process the milk and bottle it for sale.

Carron Croft

While working at the estate, I boarded with a farming family named Smart. The name of Smart in Scotland is a corruption of the name Stuart. Mr. Smart, who was well up in years, was the retired *domini*, or schoolmaster, of the one-room school in Carronbridge, a little village close to Drumlanrig Castle. I think his wife was from Dumbartonshire further north. They had several sons and a daughter. One son was living with them, and all the others had gone off to positions in various capacities in other parts of Scotland.

Their house and their farm was called Carron Croft. In Scotland, a *croft* is a small farm of one to forty-nine acres. Fifty acres or more is called a farm. Most of the farms and crofts in Scotland are on the west coast among the islands. There, the crofters make their living through keeping a few head of cattle and sheep, a few chickens, fishing—because they're all near the ocean—growing vegetable gardens for the broth which is their leading food, and growing the oats which make the oatmeal or porridge. They make their whole living off the crofts, and have very little to do with money.

Carron Croft was in the southern uplands of Dumfriesshire, which is on the border of Scotland and England. At Carron Croft, we were about fifteen miles north of the town of Dumfries, from which it was about twenty miles to the border at Gretna Green. It was very hilly country, and up on one of these hills was the farmhouse known as Carron Croft, a two-story dwelling that was three or four hundred years old. It contained just a few rooms, of which normally only the bedrooms, the bathroom, and the kitchen were used. There were some spare rooms also, and a sitting room which was very seldom used. Practically all the living took place in the kitchen, where the food was prepared and where we ate our meals, talked, and sat around the fire.

Carron Croft was the typical Scottish farmhouse. In those days, the cooking facilities in the kitchens were what they called the *inglenook*. The inglenook was a large, deep fireplace in the wall, connected by the chimney to the outside. It had a grate underneath, where hot coals would be kept burning all the time, and the food was prepared using a crane that was hung above the coals. If you wanted to fry food, a huge frying pan—sometimes they were two feet across—was swung over, and the food was fried in that. At other times a huge pot would be put over the fire for making broth. The broth pot was so large that it could contain a whole head of cabbage as well as an enormous amount of vegetables, such as potatoes, turnips, onions, carrots, leeks particularly, and all varieties of food. Sometimes a large roast of mutton would be put in the pot, and it would boil overnight, all night long. In order to serve that food from the broth, the mutton would be taken out, put on a platter, and then sliced like a roast. But the main ingredient for the

Carron Croft, a house built by the Douglasses.

broth was pearl barley. The barley made the broth thick. Sometimes even a dash of Scotch whiskey was put in.

The croft covered about three acres, and had outbuildings and a very fertile pasture. Of course, in arid New Mexico, when you turn out cattle on the range, you number how many head of cattle to the section, or 640 acres—and sometimes as few as fifteen head can be carried on one section. But in rainy, fertile Scotland, an acre alone might support the grazing of five head of cattle, so on those three acres at Carron Croft they could graze fifteen head of cattle or more. It was a nice little farm.

It was at Carron Croft, with the Smart family, that I picked up my Scottish accent, and also from the people that I worked with on the farms. There was no one there who didn't speak with the Scottish burr. They were all rustic people, and I felt very, very comfortable with them, just like I would later with the bean farmers and cowboys in the American Southwest.

When I was living at Carron Croft and working at The Drum, I would start out on my bicycle early in the morning while it was still dark, and would ride the six miles to work. In the wintertime in Scotland, it doesn't get daylight until about nine o'clock in the morning, and it gets dark about three o'clock in the afternoon; so I'd also journey home through the dark. Well, there was a spot on the road that they called The Heads, a stone monument on the side of the road that looked just like a tombstone. The monument had a lot of writing on it that I couldn't decipher, and the figure of a fish.

In the old days, Morton Castle, a neighbor to The Drum, was the home of the Douglases, a very important clan in the south of Scotland. Black Douglas, the chief, lived in Morton Castle with a wife named Agnes—Black Agnes. Everybody was terrified of the Black Douglas because he was ruthless and cruel. He was one of the famous border raiders, and used to lead a small army across the English border to raid farms and bring back cattle. These border wars went on for several centuries, and the Black Douglas became one of the legendary characters from that time on.

One day, the story goes, the Black Douglas left Morton Castle to go on one of his raids down into England, leaving Black Agnes home. They had a lackey named Edward, and Black Agnes took a shine to this young fellow. He wouldn't pay any attention to her at all, however. Black Agnes was so angered that this young man spurned her that when the Black Douglas returned, she told him that Edward had approached her and made suggestions. This put the Douglas into a rage, and he went after the poor servant, swearing he would have the boy killed.

A poet in Thornhill later wrote that the Black Douglas vowed:

> Gang fetch to me yon twa wild steeds
> Wihilk gang in knockensha
> And ere I either eat or drink
> To death I will him draw.

He ordered the two wild horses to be brought to him, and they were attached to a doubletree on a wagon. Then they brought Edward out, put a rope around his neck, and attached the rope to the wagon. Then the horses were sent running, terrified to be dragging this thing behind them. The poet continued:

> Awa, awa the frightened pair
> Still flew on wings of fear
> Along the wild and rugged road
> That leads to Durisdeer.

Durisdeer was a little village close to the Castle.

So on the horses ran, dragging the body of Edward with the rope around his neck, and at The Heads, where the monument is—that is supposed to be where Edward's head separated from his body. And, of course, there is a superstition that his ghost haunts the area around there to this day I had to ride by there on my bicycle in the dark of the morning and afternoon, and when I'd go by, I'd get a terrible feeling.

Beuchan Peter Pan

When I was working at The Drum, I got acquainted with some neighboring farmers who were raising the absolutely superb Ayrshire cattle. One of them was Morton Mains. In Scotland, a *mains* is generally the residence of a minister near a church in the village. But there was no minister around Morton Mains. Morton got that name because he was close to the ruins of Morton Castle, the castle of the Black Douglas.

Like all the farmers on the duke's estate, Morton Mains rented his farm. None of the farmers owned their farms because they were all on land long owned by the Duke of Buccleuch. Instead, they leased their farms. Their fathers had leased them, and their grandfathers, their great-grandfathers, and their great-great-grandfathers.

On these farms, they bred the cattle, they milked the cows, they shipped the milk, they made cheese in the summertime—they did everything that a dairy farm should do. The farmers had to work on Sundays, of course, because the cows had to be milked and the livestock had to be fed. But the farmers didn't work in the fields on Sundays, so there were a lot of idle hours, particularly in the afternoons.

It was the custom then that farm families would visit each other on

Carronbridge village, located below Carron Croft. I rode through the village every day on my bicycle.

Sundays. They would have tea and then go out to the cow sheds to admire the cattle and talk shop. They'd tell of the fabled ancestry of their livestock—how this one was descended from this bull, and so forth. Every calf born on those farms, and on Morton Mains in particular, was highly pedigreed, and among the very finest of the Ayrshire breed.

The families used to come to visit in what they called a governor's cart, a little cart with shafts and seats that went around the sides. The person who drove the cart would sit in the front and hold the reins, and the others would sit in the seats around the cart. The governor's cart was pulled by a pony—maybe a Highland pony or a Welsh pony—but one that was suitable for pulling that little cart.

Well, of the calves that were born, although they were all highly pedigreed, only the heifers—the female calves—were kept; these were fed milk and raised with care. But the bull calves—that was something different. There were always too many bull calves, and they couldn't do anything with them. No matter what the pedigree was, no matter what the bloodlines—as soon as a bull calf was born, they wouldn't bother with it anymore. It was disposed of.

We had a livestock feed called molassine, a very nutritious feed for dairy cattle that was made of molasses and grains of different kinds, all mixed together to make a very sticky dairy food. The molasses was imported from the British West Indies or from Africa, and was the cheapest of the molasses; it was just for livestock and not for human consumption. They bought the molassine in one-hundred-pound sacks, and always kept the sack after it was empty, thinking they might need to use it for something.

Now, in that area, in Thornhill, there was a sausage factory run by a man named Soosanny. He had a cart pulled by a draft horse, and over the cart was a metal net. He used to ride around in that cart from farm to farm to see if they had any pigs or excess bull calves for sale. One day—it must have been a Saturday—one of the cows at Morton Mains had a calf, a bull calf. When Mr. Osborn of Morton Mains went out and looked at the calf, he decided that the calf wouldn't be of any use.

The local custom, if one wanted to get rid of a calf, was to get an empty molassine sack and put the poor, pathetic calf in that sack and tie up the top so that only its head was sticking out. It couldn't move because it was in that sticky, old molassine sack; it could only wait for Soosanny and the trip to the sausage factory. It used to break my heart, because I loved animals, to see those little creatures treated that way. Soosanny would buy the calf, throw it in the cart with all the pigs he had bought, and take it to Thornhill, where he'd kill it and grind it up into sausage.

Near Morton Mains was a farm called The Beuchan, run by two old maids, Miss Allen and Miss Allen. They were sisters. On the Sunday after this little calf was born, the Misses Allen thought they'd go over and have tea with Morton Mains. After tea, they went out as usual to admire the Morton Mains cattle. When they came into the byre, here the Misses Allen saw this little calf, tied up in this sticky sack of molassine, waiting for Soosanny to come by the next day. They went over to it, these two old maids, and they looked at its head, and they examined its eyes and ears and nose; and they said to Mr. Osborn, "Would you let us see that calf?" Mr. Osborn untied the sack, and the poor little thing was pulled out—it hadn't even had time to learn to stand up because it had been in the sack all the time.

The Misses Allen looked at its markings, and then they started talking to each other. They said, "Mr. Osborn, would you sell us that calf?"

Mr. Osborn said, "Well, I was hoping that Soosanny would come tomorrow and take it away."

They said, "We'd like to buy him. Maybe we'll want to keep him for a bull."

Then he said, "Well, there's no quality about it."

"Oh, we like the little calf," said the Misses Allen.

They said they would pay Mr. Osborn if he would sell them the calf, and a price was agreed upon. When the Misses Allen were ready to leave, instead of putting the little thing back in the molassine sack, Mr. Osborn just bound its legs so that they could take him in the governor's cart. They took him over to The Beuchan, their farm, and put him among their herd. This must have been around 1912 or 1913, just before World War I started. The little bull calf was fed milk, and he responded and put on weight; and they groomed him and made him look just like a bull that they might sell.

Now, the calf had been registered. Mr. Osborn had told them who the sire was and who the cow was—the registered names and the registered numbers. The cattle on all those farms were registered beef or dairy cattle, and on the registration form, the name of the farm was listed first. So they re-registered this little calf under the name of "Beuchan Peter Pan." And after the calf was pretty well along in age— not full grown, but not a little helpless thing like he had been—it came time that they wanted to profit from him. So they sold him to a dealer who was collecting the finest Ayrshire cattle he could find to ship to the United States. And this little bull, Beuchan Peter Pan, was sold and shipped across the Atlantic to America.

A scene at Thornhill.

If those two little old ladies, the Misses Allen, had not come along and seen that calf, he would have been delivered to Soosanny the next day and taken to the sausage factory. Instead, in 1915, at the Panama Pacific Exposition, in San Diego, Beuchan Peter Pan was named the World Champion Ayrshire.

Waterside of Keir

It was sometime in 1921, after I had worked at The Drum for a while, that I changed over to another farm near Drumlanrig Castle. This farm was near the little village of Keir. There was a broad stream that went through there which would be called practically a river here in the United States. It was called Keir Water, and the farm was called Waterside of Keir. There I had much more experience, both in the raising of Ayrshire cattle and in dairy farming.

I also had a lot of field experience at Waterside—more than I had at The Drum—such as the growing of crops used to feed the cattle. he big feed in Scotland for cattle was not so much oats as the oat straw, which has a very high nutritive value. Wheat bran is considered important here, but in Scotland, wheat was considered to have no nutritive value at all. Wheat straw was burned. But when the oats were harvested, the oat straw was stacked, and the cattle ate it.

They generally rotated crops on Scottish farms. They had barley, and roots such as turnips—big Swedish turnips. They call them rutabagas in this country, but because of the short season here, they grow just to a medium size. Oats were important too, for the straw particularly, and for making into oatmeal for home use. And then there was ryegrass hay, which was plowed in to give more humus to the soil.

I loved Waterside, and I loved the cattle. When I got up in the morning at Carron Croft, the Smarts would have breakfast ready for me—the usual Scottish breakfast of tea, oatmeal, eggs with bacon or kippered herring, and scones and jam. Then I'd get on my bicycle at about four A.M. and ride to Waterside to help with the milking.

At Waterside, I had a lot of experience in cheese making all during the summertime. During the winter, the milk was put into cans and shipped into Glasgow, but in the summertime, all the milk went into cheese.

I made a sixty-pound cheddar every day, and a fourteen-pound Stilton. The cheese was made in the old-fashioned way; there was no processing about it. It was made in the vat, where the rennet was put into the milk and the curds were drained off. The whey from the vat went down a pipe to a sort of cistern at the pigpens, and it was fed to the pigs. (And if you want to eat delicious pork, get a Scottish pig raised on whey.) But the cheeses that I made—both of them were put into the cheese presses, wrapped in cheesecloth, and then taken to a storage room where they were kept at a certain temperature. They were put on shelves, and every day for about four months, they would be turned over. After four months, it was the most delicious cheddar you ever had. The cheddar was yellow, and the Stilton a little whitish. You could take a slice of that Stilton cheese, hold it up to a light, and see little blue veins going through it; that meant it was a perfect cheese.

Kirkpatrick MacMillan

The village of Keir is famous all through Scotland, and also in other parts of the world, because of a village blacksmith from the mid-1800s, whose name was Kirkpatrick MacMillan. Not only did he do the shoeing of horses and the repairing of farm implements, and everything else that a blacksmith usually does, but he liked to experiment on things made of wood.

There was one little wooden contraption that he made in his shop in about 1840. It had two circular things on short axles, little pedals where you could put your feet, and then something like bars where you could put your hands. And you could sit on this thing. He used to go out of his shop on it, and ride pedaling up the road, and people called him Daft Pate—crazy Pate, because of that.

Then after a while, he got so involved in his invention that he decided to pedal that thing from Keir to Glasgow up the Kilmarnock Road, and people came out from the villages to watch Daft Pate go by.

There was a man at nearby Kilmarnock named MacCall who was terribly interested in this contraption, and he improved on it by making it out of metal instead of wood. He sort of capitalized on this thing, and Daft Pate went back to his blacksmith shop and wasn't heard from much after that.

When I was at Waterside, I used to go out and bring the cattle in for the afternoon milking. Where the cattle grazed was pretty close to the village of Keir, and I'd often see people coming into the graveyard there to visit. A lot of people came there—none of them from Keir—and many carried bouquets of flowers and put them on one of the graves there. All the people of Keir, as well as myself, wondered what the devil they were doing that for.

There had once been an old lady called Eppie in Keir whose head was not quite right. She was a little bit "daft," as they used to say. We thought that Keir couldn't produce anyone more famous than Eppie, who used to say the most ridiculous things. She believed in phantoms and things like that! People used to ask Eppie what her phantoms looked like, and Eppie would say, "Oh, they were for all the world like little ducks." So we all thought that the visitors of the graveyard were coming to see this local eccentric's grave. Then, finally, we learned that everyone was coming to see the grave of Kirkpatrick MacMillan—the inventor of the bicycle.

Leave Taking

I finally completed my apprenticeship in horticulture and animal husbandry, and by New Year's Day of 1923, I was prepared to go abroad. Now my people suggested that because I was interested in beef cattle, I might go to Argentina. There was a British company there called the Bovril Company. Bovril is a food used all over the British world, particularly in England. It looks like syrup. You take a spoon of it, put it in a pot of boiling water, and it makes a sort of beef broth. It's delicious. The company also put up canned corned beef like that bought at any supermarket here today.

At first, I thought that it would be ideal to be out there on the *estancias* of Argentina with the gauchos. The Bovril Company was managed by Scots in every department, including the *estancias*, and it would have been fine. I would have been doing a lot of horseback riding there. But it didn't appeal to me because of my fondness for animals. I had heard that the gauchos were very cruel to horses, cattle, and any kind of livestock. And another thing—I would have to put in a two-year apprenticeship in the Bovril packing houses in Buenos Aires before I could go to the ranches. The thought of being in a slaughterhouse, with my feelings toward animals—no, that wouldn't do. So I had to give that up. It would have been a wonderful life, working on the *estancias* and going back and forth to Scotland, but the slaughterhouse and the gaucho cruelty to animals didn't appeal to me—especially the slaughterhouse part.

So I would have to go to a British colony. My family decided on British Columbia, and made arrangements for me to spend two years on a fruit farm there. I was to go to a little place called Kelowna, which is on a beautiful lake in the Okanagan Valley. All around the lake were fruit farms with all kinds of fruit—cherries, plums, peaches, and apples, mostly Jonathans. I was to establish myself there first, and then take trips up to the Fraser River Valley to look around for a cattle ranch. It would first be the fruit in the Okanagan Valley, and then the cattle in the upper Fraser River Valley. My family was to get the property in the Fraser River Valley after I had finished the fruit farming.

I felt equal to the task. I had had a lot of riding experience on my grandfather's shooting estate up in Perthshire. Of course, my experience was on polo ponies with an English saddle, not on cutting horses with stock saddles. But I loved horseback riding. The plan appealed to me—the combination of riding horses and raising beef cattle up in the Fraser River Valley. And the cattle ranches there are as good as they are anywhere in the world.

In February of 1923, I sailed out of Glasgow on the *Berengaria*, a ship on the Cunard line, traveling second class to avoid having to dress for dinner.

Although the New York shoreline wasn't nearly as impressive then as it must be now, when I saw the piers on the waterfront, it took me back to when I was almost a baby, when my mother used to carry me in her arms down to the ships. But now my mother was no longer with me. I was alone again, on my way across the continent to British Columbia.

First, however, I stayed for a time with my Aunt Marguerite in New York. She had married an Englishman named Reuben, and now they had two children. After the snobbery of my relatives in England, my aunt and uncle were a welcome relief, they were so open and kindly. I also spent a few weeks working on a fruit farm outside New York City. Then one day, while staying with my aunt and uncle, we got to talking about the sea. I told them that I would like to take a job on a ship, if only for a short while. My aunt said, "Why don't you go see Mr. Lilly, at Norton Lilly and Company?" They had been the agents for my father's steamship company.

I thought, "Gee, what a fine idea. I'll do that."

So I wrote to Norton Lilly, and said that I would like to meet Mr. Lilly. I told them who I was, and who my father was, and they said to come down to the office.

I told Mr. Lilly, who had been a great friend of my father, that I'd like to take a voyage on a ship someplace—anywhere—and that I'd like to get on a Bucknall boat. He said, "Well, unfortunately, on the

46

Bucknall steamers, the crews are all native—Indians." Only the officers were non-native; they were British.

Mr. Lilly said, "I don't think you could get onto a Bucknall boat because of that, but there are others. We represent the Isthmian line, and they go all over the world." The Isthmian line included the United States Steel Corporation's steamers—freight boats.

"I'll tell you what," he said. "I'll give you a letter of introduction to Captain Donnelly, the marine superintendent of the Isthmian line." Captain Donnelly had the same job that my father had with Bucknall. "Captain Donnelly might have something on," Mr. Lilly said.

So I saw Captain Donnelly, and told him what I wanted. Like Mr. Lilly, Captain Donnelly had known my father, and he agreed to let me on. "All right," he said, "but I know darned well you won't stay with it."

I told him, "I just want one voyage—one trip." \I didn't know where the ship would be going, but it would be going somewhere, and that's all I cared about.

Captain Donnelly was successful in finding a ship that needed a hand, and I signed on. It was a big freighter, called the *Howick Hall*, that was supposed to sail from New York to Boston. From Boston it would haul freight across the seas, to wherever the freight was destined. They didn't even yet know where the ship would go from Boston; they wouldn't know until it arrived there.

I was just a deckhand on the *Howick Hall*, and as it turned out, for only a few days.

It was a terrible experience. The crew were all Filipinos and Spaniards—along with some Hawaiians—and they all spoke Spanish and wouldn't have anything to do with anybody who was European—not even the son of an executive of a major shipping line. I didn't like the experience at all, and so I said to myself, "I'm not going to stay with this." I had been warned back in port, "If you sign on it from Boston, you're fixed for the voyage—wherever it goes and back again." So I got off in Boston. Captain Donnelly was right. It was no fun at all, and I was finished as a sailor.

After that, in August, I decided to make an appointment with the man I was to see at Kelowna, British Columbia, a retired Presbyterian minister. Living with a minister didn't appeal to me very much; it sounded stuffy. But I had my mission.

I got a train ticket to San Francisco, thinking to go by boat from there north to British Columbia. I could have taken the Canadian Pacific from New York, but I decided I'd like to see the Southwest on my way across the country. I probably wouldn't be headed back to New York again, and if I were to go back, I'd probably be taking the Northern Pacific or the Chicago, Milwaukee and St. Paul—one of the northern routes. So I decided to buy a ticket on the New York Central to Chicago, go on to Santa Fe, and from there on to San Francisco. I thought that would suit me fine.

I changed onto the Santa Fe at Dearborn Station in Chicago, taking the *Missionary*, one of the very best of that line. But instead of taking the Pullman car, I bought a ticket on the day coach because I didn't want more luxury. I was sick by then of hearing all about nobility and our famous ancestry in Scotland.

In Kansas City, a man got onto the train and sat beside me. He was a cattleman, going back home to Clovis, New Mexico, after selling a bunch of cattle at the market in Kansas City. We got along well, and talked as the train headed further and further west into the plains of Kansas and the drier lands of Oklahoma before crossing into Texas and New Mexico. I knew that this was where the ranching country was, and I liked the openness of it—and my companion sensed this. Before we got to Clovis, just across the line from Farwell, Texas, he said to me, "You know, you can go into ranching in British Columbia, all right, but there you'll have to feed cattle all winter, and you'll have to ride sleighs to do so. Now, look at this country. Look at the grass we have. We don't have to do that here."

When we got into the station at Clovis, August 15, 1923, it was mid-morning, and I saw saddle ponies tied up at the station, and cowboys loitering about, and I thought to myself, "If this is beef-cattle raising, this is for me!" I picked up my suitcase, got off, and watched the train move down the tracks on its way to San Francisco.

My companion then told me, "If you want to see some good ranching country, go down to Roswell. The train leaves at twelve noon." I decided to take his advice.

New Mexico, First Views

The train got into Roswell a short time after leaving Clovis. I didn't know where to go, but I saw this building, the Roswell Hotel, and went in and said, "I'd like a room." I was told, "Very well. We have a nice room here, and it's fifty cents a night." I thought it would be sort of a flophouse for that price, but it wasn't. It was a nice hotel, a real country-style house with several rooms for rent at fifty cents per night. In the back they had housekeeping rooms for seventy-five cents a week. They didn't give you any blankets, but there was a little cot in the room, and a kerosene range you could cook your meals on. The hotel was run by a man named Morisky. I don't know where he came from, but he spoke with a foreign accent, probably Polish or something like that. That was my first home in New Mexico, and I stayed there for about a week.

After checking into the hotel, I went over and talked to a man at the chamber of commerce. I told him about my family in Scotland, the money I had, and my interest in beef cattle. He was an awfully nice fellow; I think his name was Claude Simpson. I told him that I'd been on my way to British Columbia, and he said, "I'm glad you didn't make it, and that you decided to stay here." He encouraged me by saying, "I'd advise you to get into cattle raising around here. That would be ideal for you." Then I went over and talked to the banker, and he said the same thing. So I said to myself, "I'm going to go back to Scotland and see if my people would be interested in setting me up in cattle or sheep ranching here in New Mexico."

Roswell was delightful. There was a little park by the courthouse with benches that old-time cowboys liked to sit on, and they would strike up a conversation with anybody. They were friendly, and I liked that.

I didn't know anything about Roswell except that it was cattle country, but some of the old-timers I met that week really instructed me.

They told me that the town was started in the late 1860s, when John Chisum, later called the "Pecos Cattle King," brought his herd of cattle to Fort Sumner and then claimed all the land from Fort Sumner down to Carlsbad, over 160 miles away. The city of Carlsbad today is an old Chisum cow camp. Just south of Roswell, Chisum put in his South Spring Ranch, a big farm and ranch.

Later I would learn more, sitting in the park or hanging around Second and Main, where the local cowboys met, and of course by working on ranches in the area. But for now, I was simply enchanted, and ready to go back to Scotland to tell my people about the great opportunities to be found in this wonderful country.

Before going, however, I decided that I'd like to see a bit more of the Southwest. The man in the bank had said, "Why don't you take a trip west of here, up the road there over to Tularosa and down to Alamogordo?" And he said, "Then go down to El Paso. You can get a train in El Paso back to wherever you want to go." I asked him, "How do I go there?"

"Well," he said, "you could take a train, but you won't see any of the country. Why don't you get out on the road? There are salesmen going by all the time. Pick up a ride with one of them, and they'll take you at least on to Ruidoso or Tularosa, and then you can go down to Alamogordo." And he added, "Why don't you see Arizona while you're here?" I told him, "I think that's just what I'll do."

While I was loitering around Roswell my last day there, not really in any hurry to get anywhere, I walked down Main Street to what was called the PV Wagon Yard—PV for Pecos Valley. There I saw a sight that appealed to me very much. A bunch of homesteaders had come in by covered wagon, and had put up at the wagon yard. Their horses were in corrals at the yard, and they were camped there. The women wore sunbonnets, and gingham skirts right down to their ankles. They were barefooted, and some were smoking little clay pipes. All the others—men, women, and children alike—held a chew of tobacco in their jaws or dip under their lips.

I got to talking with these folks, and found that they had come from Oklahoma, from up around McAlester, and their name, in fact, was McAlester—a good Scottish name. I said I was going to go on west tomorrow along the highway, and that I might catch a ride with a salesman. One of them said, "Come on with us!"

"No, thanks," I said, "I'm going to get a ride with a salesman," thinking the ride might be smoother and faster that way.

Traveling Around

I spent that night at the hotel, and walked down to the highway with my suitcase the next morning, hoping to flag a ride to El Paso and all those points in between that the banker had told me about—Ruidoso, Tularosa, and Alamogordo. The "highway" turned out to be a terrible stretch of deep-rutted dirt, but at least it looked well traveled.

Apparently, however, you had to wait a long while before a car would come along that road, because I sat there a long time with no success. Then, finally, I saw something approaching slowly in the distance— three covered wagons, followed by extra horses being driven behind them.

One of the wagons eventually pulled up in front of me, and the old guy driving it said, "Howdy." Sure enough, he was one of the McAlesters from back in the wagon yard. If he recognized me, though, he didn't give any indication."

"Well, hello," I said. "Where are you going?"

"We're going to Muscular." He meant "Mescalero," but it came out a little different. "What are you doing here?"

"I'm waiting for a ride. I'm hoping maybe a salesman will come by."

"You might wait a long time. Go on, get on here."

I took him up on his offer and sat beside him on the driver's seat. When it got dark, we camped by Picacho Hill above the Hondo Valley, about forty miles west of Roswell. The women built a campfire and fried up okra and salt pork for dinner, which we ate along with cold corn pone and coffee. They threw out some blankets for me to sleep on, and that night, for the first time in my life, I slept on the ground. And it was fine.

We continued the journey the next day, riding down into the Hondo Valley. When we got to Hondo, McAlester said, "We're going up that way, up to Reahdosa," meaning Ruidoso. "Come on, if you wanta."

I said, "No, thanks. I'll see if I can't get a ride here." I walked over to the store at Hondo, which was run by a man named Rose—another Scottish clan name. He was renting little rooms up above—it was a little hotel—and I asked if I could stay, and if breakfast, dinner, supper were available. I could and they were, so I spent that night in Hondo.

Early the next morning, I got up and went downstairs, and in the store was a salesman. I told him I was traveling west, and I wondered if I could get a ride.

"Well, I'm going down that way," he said. "Be glad to take you." After he completed his sales and order-taking—I believe he sold grocery items and tobacco—he said, "Well, I'm all ready to go." So I picked up my suitcase, and we started out in his Model T. The next stop was Ruidoso, some twenty miles west.

Except for the Rio Ruidoso (Noisy River) that runs through it, Ruidoso was a sleepy little mountain village in 1923. There was a store with a hand-operated gasoline pump, an old mill, and a few cabins built on stilts on the side of the hill. That was all Ruidoso was. They were talking about building a lodge there, but they hadn't yet. Now, of course, there are motels, condominiums, resort hotels, and dozens of restaurants. I liked Ruidoso very much indeed the way it was back then—but not as much as the plains.

At our next stop, in Mescalero, between the White and Sacramento mountains, the salesman stopped first at the trading post and then went down to the Benton Store, run by Jim McNatt. This was where I saw Indians for the first time—Apaches, mostly men and children. The men wore headbands around long, shaggy hair, and were dressed in ragged shirts, Levis, and what looked like pajamas. The kids ran around practically naked. All of them seemed dirty. Things have changed for the better since then in some ways. Now the Mescaleros are one of the nation's richest tribes, with good houses, a fancy resort, and a ski run.

From there the salesman and I went on down to Tularosa, a ranching and farming town frequently raided in the past by Apaches, and then down to Alamogordo in the desert. It was getting dark by the time we arrived there, and pretty close to that time a train was coming in from the east. So I said good-bye to the salesman and bought a ticket for El Paso.

El Paso was a dirty, dusty, rotten, filthy town, like all border towns at the time, and I just loved it. The Mexicans dressed just like I'd seen in pictures, with serapes draped over their shoulders and great big sombreros on their heads. Some of the men had pigtails down their backs. I stayed for a few days, putting up in a hotel with rooms upstairs—nothing fancy—and then decided to see what the country was like west of there.

I didn't really have any idea where to go, but I bought a ticket on the El Paso and Southwestern Railroad, bound for Yuma, Arizona, with stops at Deming and Lordsburg, New Mexico, and Tucson, Arizona.

This was a different country—desert country, flat and dry—and I thought to myself that I could live here, too. But I wasn't so sure about the heat, and by the time I got to Yuma, I didn't think that I wanted to go any further. I saw yellow hills to the west of Yuma that didn't look very inviting, and I asked someone on the street, "What's over there?"

"That's California. It's on the other side of the river."

Well, I didn't want to go to California—the hills looked like someone's version of hell, and California meant I was getting closer to San Francisco and British Columbia, which by now I wanted nothing to do with. So I bought a ticket back to El Paso, where I decided I would spend a day or two before heading back east and to Scotland.

Back in El Paso, I got acquainted with some men who were sitting in the hotel lobby. One man asked me, "What do you want to see now?"

I thought for a moment, and then said, "I want to see Texas. I'd like to go on to Fort Worth and Dallas before I go back across the Atlantic again."

He said, "Well, why don't you? But you won't see it by just looking out the window of a train."

"No, you're right," I said. "I've seen a lot of the country from a train, but I'd like to see it differently."

The man replied, "Get out on the road, then, and hook you a ride the same as you did when you went out of Roswell. Some salesman will pick you up. And why don't you get rid of that old suitcase, and get you something to put on your back?"

That struck me as good advice, so the next morning, I took all of my belongings out of the suitcase, put them into a knapsack, and left my suitcase at the hotel.

I walked a long way before my first ride came along, far outside the city limits and pretty close to Ysleta, twelve miles from town. It wasn't a Model T this time, but a truck; not a big truck—they didn't have big diesels in those days—maybe a two-ton. "I'll give you a ride," the driver said, but if you want to go to Fort Worth and Dallas, you'll have to get off at Sierra Blanca because the road splits there. One road goes down to the Rio Grande Valley, and the other one goes your way." Sierra Blanca was only about one hundred miles, but it was a start, so I hopped on the truck.

When I got off, I didn't see anyplace I could stay, but I managed to meet a young fellow there about my own age who was an enterprising sort. I asked him, "What are you doing here?"

"I'm going to Fort Worth," he replied.

"That's where I want to go, too," I said. "I'm thinking of taking the train."

"I'm taking the train, too," my new friend said, "but damned if I'm going to take any passenger train and pay my way. I'm not going to ride any cushions. I'm going to catch a freight. Why don't you come with me?"

We waited around the yard for a spell, and finally a freight train came in from the west, going east. It had boxcars, coal cars or gondolas, flat cars—every kind of freight train car. My friend said, "See that one there? When the train stops, we'll catch that."

When the train came to a stop, we walked out to it, and there seemed to be nobody around, not even a brakey. The train was just standing there, so we climbed up into one of the gondolas and sat down. The train then did some maneuvering backward and forward while it was being off-loaded and loaded, and then there was a big jerk and we started off to the east toward Dallas and Fort Worth.

We squatted down in the gondola, and after a while one of the brakeys discovered us. "What are you fellows doing here?" he said. "Get off at the next stop." I forget where that stop was, but when the train pulled in, we didn't move. At that point, they took on a bunch of Mexican section hands. Boy, were they a tough-looking bunch. We sat on one end of the car, and they sat on the other, talking by themselves in Spanish.

Then the brakey came in again after the train had started, and he said, "Oh, you're still here?"

"Yeah, we're still here."

"All right," he said, "gimme a dollar and I'll let you ride."

I reached in my pocket, got my wallet out to get some money, and the brakey practically threw himself on me. He said, "That'll be a dollar," and I pulled a dollar from my wallet and gave it to him.

"Put that wallet back," the brakey told me in a low voice. "Don't let those guys over there know you've got any money on you at all."

I asked, "What would happen?"

"The train would get going," he replied, "and they would take your wallet from you and pitch you over the side of the train."

That was the closest to death I had ever been. After that, I kept quiet about the wallet.

The brakey told us, "I'm going as far as Midland." That was a little less than halfway from El Paso to Dallas. "You can ride as long as I'm here, but somebody else will be on here after Midland, so you'd better get off there." When the train finally pulled into Midland, we jumped off and we walked over toward the depot, but we were intercepted by the yard policeman, the law enforcement of the railroad yard.

"You come in on that train?" he asked.

"Yes, we did."

"All right," he said, "I'll tell you what I'll do. I'll put you up for the night at the depot here."

That sounded a lot better to us than jail—until he locked us up in the colored waiting room with no food and no water. We were in there all night, scared to death and not knowing what would happen to us.

In the morning, the yard policeman set us free, however, and my friend and I walked down to a café to get some breakfast.

"This is all I want of riding freight trains," I told him. "I'm buying a ticket this time." And we parted company.

I rode to Dallas on the Texas and Pacific, only to find that Dallas could hold my interest for only a day or two. I bought a ticket out of there on the Missouri, Kansas and Texas line, going north to Atoka, in eastern Oklahoma, with lush, green hills that appealed to me. Then I went on into St. Louis, which, after falling in love with New Mexico, was just another big American city to me. I didn't like it at all. Nor did America east of there excite me. So I traveled nonstop to New York; and there, after a little while, I boarded a steamer on the Anchor line, the *Columbia*, and sailed to Glasgow. It was late September 1923.

Disinherited

The great question that I carried with me on the voyage across the Atlantic was, "Will my uncle and aunt agree to let me start a family ranching business in New Mexico instead of British Columbia?"

They would not. My uncle said, "If you want to be an American, you'll have to go on your own. We won't help you. If you had gone on to Canada as you were supposed to, we would have invested in a ranch there. If you want to be an American, you are not with us anymore."

Right then, I had to decide whether to become an American or remain a Scotsman in a family that was almost completely anglicized. The choice should have been a terrible one, but it was somehow not difficult to make. It was made even easier when Uncle David said that he would pay my passage back to the United States; and he promised to pay me a remittance twice a year from Grandfather's estate. I also expected to eventually inherit the bulk of the estate, since after my uncle's death I would be the sole male heir of the Sinclairs.

The inheritance, however, never arrived.

When my grandfather died, he had left me around a thousand pounds—$5,000 in American money—which I was to get when I was thirty years old. According to the will, I would receive the residue when Uncle David died. Grandfather was very wealthy, and I was in line for hundreds of thousands, eventually. But when I made my decision to go to America, the trustees—my Aunt Vida and Uncle David—conspired to cut me off.

They did so ingeniously. They simply squandered the inheritance. They took trips to Cannes, to Monte Carlo, and to Australia. They gambled, they traveled, and they spent virtually all of that money—not only my money, but also my Aunt Mary's inheritance.

I finally managed to get some of the inheritance decades later, when I was in Rodeo, New Mexico, in 1963. It seems there was $30,000 left that the treasury solicitor didn't know what to do with, and a firm that located heirs found me through Aunt Mary's daughters. The firm wrote to me, and said it had found this sum of money in London and was trying to find the heir of David Sinclair, my grandfather. Was I that heir? I told them that I was, all right, and to prove it I sent them my birth certificate, my father's and mother's marriage certificate, and other documents; and finally it was proved to their satisfaction that I was who I claimed to be.

The $30,000 that was left from the estate was supposed to be divided between myself and my cousins—by then, my Aunt Mary had died. I was to get so much, and the others would get a half of what I got; if I got $10,000, for example, then they would get $5,000 to divide among the four of them. Well, the firm that contacted me said that their fee was a third of the total amount. That left about $20,000. But before it was all cleared, there were lawyers involved—English lawyers, Scottish lawyers, and American lawyers in New York and London. I ended up with $800, and my four cousins got $400 to split four ways.

Out of hundreds of thousands.

It was still September when I sailed back to America on the *Assyria*, another Anchor ship. I was ignorant of my uncle and aunt's scheming, but knew, no matter what, that I wanted nothing more to do with them. I wanted to be free, to be on my own. And I was happy because I'd found a place I wanted to live—New Mexico.

Diamond A headquarters in Roswell.
(Photo by Rodden Studios, Roswell).

Cowboy Riding Country

W hen I got back to Roswell later that fall, I knew that I had to give up any ambition of owning a ranch and find a job to support myself. What was I going to do? I wanted to work with livestock, of course, but the only job I was able to find at first was chopping cotton in the Pecos Valley near Roswell—and then as the season changed, picking cotton. It was hard work.

Finally, I said to myself, "This isn't my kind of life. I want to get into the beef business."

I found a job on a ranch at Lake Arthur, in a valley south of Roswell. It wasn't a riding job; it was a job making an earthen water tank with a couple of mules and a fresno plow. The fellow who ran the ranch said to me one day, "What you need is a riding outfit."

He advised me to go into Roswell and buy what I needed, so I did—a saddle, a saddle blanket, bridle and bits, a good lariat, a tarp for a bed, and some blankets to go with the tarp to make up a bedroll; and of course I also bought clothes—a slicker, khaki trousers and shirts, boots, gloves, and a hat.

After that I got more work on ranches, still mostly odd jobs, it's true—milking cows, turning cream separators, taking care of hogs— but also such work as riding out to the pasture to check on the cattle. Things were coming together.

Then, in the summer of 1926, I got a job on the Diamond A Ranch, west of Roswell, run by the Bloom Land and Cattle Company.

The Diamond A Ranch

In Roswell, I had met two fellows who wanted to work for the Diamond A, and one of them said, "Why don't you come out with us and ask Ed Bloom for a job?" Bloom, the foreman at the headquarters of the Diamond A, hired me on at $35 a month. I drove there in a 1918 Glide that I'd bought recently. Later I bought my first horse, a buckskin dun named Kid, from Sam Burgner, the foreman of the Circle Diamond, the horse ranch of the Bloom Land and Cattle Company. I paid $12 for Kid.

The Diamond A was by far the biggest ranch in that part of the country—about 450 sections, or 288,000 acres. It started near Picacho, up in the Hondo Valley, and followed the Hondo River east. Then it branched off southeastward to just outside Artesia, fifty miles from Picacho. It was twelve miles at its widest point, somewhere in the middle of the range, and one mile at its narrowest points, up by Picacho and down toward Artesia.

The Bloom Land and Cattle Company not only operated this Diamond A, but they operated another Diamond A up at Wagon Mound, New Mexico. That was also a big ranch, but not as big as the one I worked on. Then they had another Diamond A up by Rocky Ford, Colorado, and yet another, a large lease on the Rosebud Sioux Reservation in South Dakota. I think they also had a ranch in Saskatchewan, Canada, but that was just for raising horses, I believe.

That year, there was a terrible drought in South Dakota, and they had to move a lot of the cattle on the Rosebud to their ranches down south. Otherwise they wouldn't have had enough feed for them. So a tremendous shipment of cattle came down from South Dakota to Roswell in railroad cars, and they were driven onto our range. As a result, there were fifteen thousand mother cows and about seven thousand calves on the range that year that needed rounding up and branding. The range was so large that it took three chuck wagons on those roundups to keep the men supplied with bacon and beans, fried potatoes, biscuits, rice and raisins, dried fruit—and cup after strong cup of Best Breakfast Call coffee.

At that time, the Bloom Land and Cattle Company was also trying to improve the quality of its beef cattle, so they had purchased ninety very expensive registered Hereford bull calves. They were put out in a pasture near the headquarters that was called The River Pasture because the Hondo River ran down the middle of it. It was well watered, and had good grass.

Ed Egger, Joe Bean, and myself were put in charge of them. I still have a photograph of me holding the prize bull of all the ninety with a

My car, a Glide, with my dog Tige perched on the hood.
Diamond A Ranch, 1926.

halter. Cap Mossman, the manager of the Diamond A, paid five hundred dollars for that calf, a lot of money in those days.

The Diamond A was hard work—seven days a week of getting up in the dark and coming in after dark, and no days off except every six weeks or so. But the work appealed to me. It was the bunkhouse that bored me to death.

At night, we'd come in and roll our bedrolls out on the wooden floor; it was really simple living, and I liked that part of it. But the bunkhouses were filthy, and they stank—cigarette ashes everywhere, and tobacco juice on the stove. One cowboy, named Davis, was celebrated for being lousy and for always having a dose of the clap. Nobody would let him sleep in their bed with them. I did once, not knowing his reputation. Afterward, the other fellows told me, "He's lousy, he's got the clap, he's got the crabs, and just about everything else you can think of." I had to air out my bedroll. But I didn't catch anything.

And the talk! For the most part, the cowboys in the bunkhouse weren't very educated people. They knew horses and cattle, of course, but the talk was mostly about sports—baseball, football, and rodeo— or about jobs they'd had on other ranches, and the women in Roswell, mostly prostitutes they knew. I just wasn't interested.

There were exceptions to this rule, of course. Long before my time, Gene Rhodes worked on the Diamond A. He's best known today as Eugene Manlove Rhodes, the author of *Paso por Aquí*, one of the classic novels of the Southwest. He also wrote for the *Saturday Evening Post*. Then there was Dick Halliday, who rode into the Diamond A one day while I was working there, and put up in our bunkhouse.

Halliday rode in trailing two horses, one of them carrying his canvas bed and the other his pack saddle with all his possessions. He was an old-time Western writer for the pulp field, writing for such magazines as *Western Stories* and *Triple X*. He rode up to the ranch, and he told us he was going to stay there for a while because he had seen Captain Mossman, the general manager of the Diamond A in Roswell. Dick Halliday, of course, knew all about Mossman. He had probably written about him several times; Mossman was famous as a former Arizona ranger who had captured the Mexican bandit Chacon down in Mexico and brought him back to Arizona to be hanged.

Mossman had told him, "Why don't you go out to the Diamond A and stay out there?" He said, "We got a good cook there. We got a bunkhouse you can throw your bedroll down in, and you'll be in the company of cowboys—just what you're looking for. Go on out there and spend a few nights if you want to, or spend all winter."

So along came Dick Halliday. He unloaded his pack horse and his bedroll, putting the bedroll in the bunkhouse and his horses in the corral to feed on the haystack, and he set up shop. In his pack bags, he had his typewriter, several copies of all the pulp magazines that he had written for, and paper—all he needed to write some stories.

Halliday was writing for the pulps at one cent a word. He would write stories of about six thousand words each—or about $60 a story.

In 1926, you could live beautifully on that. He just rattled off stories while he was at the Diamond A.

The cowboys had a lot of fun with Halliday. He was of the West—he had the cowboy in his blood, and he had horses—but he wasn't earning his thirty-five or forty dollars a month the way the cowboys did. He earned that, and more, writing. In a way, he was sort of an alien there, but my friend Ed Egger and I took a shine to him. I could talk to Halliday about things I couldn't talk to the other cowboys about.

Halliday had been in the Boer War in South Africa at the turn of the century, when Britain fought for South Africa and South Africa became a colony, and he told me stories about that. He also knew my father's steamship line, which went from New York to London, from London to South Africa—to Cape Town and the Cape ports—and then into the Mediterranean, down the Suez Canal, and to islands off the coast of Africa. He knew all the ships.

Halliday stayed with us for the winter, and then moved on. He was the first writer I knew in New Mexico.

I took one break while I was at the Diamond A, at the end of 1926. They were going to have the big livestock show at the Chicago Stockyard. They called it the International Livestock Exposition, and it was one of the biggest in the country. They had livestock from Canada and all over—not the cowboy kind of cattle, but real thoroughbreds—pedigreed, registered cattle. I went to that exhibition, and walked from one stall to the next, and talked with the keepers. Most of the keepers were Scots from Canada, and I was so impressed with that. I went from one stall to the other, looking at the Shorthorns and the Galloways and the Aberdeen Angus, and all of the cattle I was familiar with—the registered Herefords, and every breed you could think of. And the horses, the wonderful, big draft horses that I knew so thoroughly—Clydesdales and Belgians and Shires and the huge Percherons. That was the most wonderful exhibition!

Years later, when I was really working as a writer, I was signed by *Holiday Magazine*, which was one of the Curtis magazines of that time, and a very important one. I went to Cheyenne to cover the Cheyenne Frontier Days Rodeo, and I was absolutely bored to death. I saw those acrobats coming out and riding those bucking horses and getting bucked off, and I saw wild-cow-milking contests. And I compared it with that wonderful exhibition that I went to in 1926. I was just bored stiff. Livestock appealed to me, but rodeo didn't appeal to me at all.

Riding Chuck Line

I left the Diamond A in 1927 and had to get another job. There had been a big stir at the ranch, and Ed Bloom was fired. He and Cap Mossman just didn't get along. A whole bunch of us quit; Walter Coleman from Roswell was coming in to replace him, and we knew we wouldn't get along with him. I decided to ride chuck line, going from ranch to ranch looking for work, if there was any work. So I got on my little dun pony, and from then on, I felt I was free to go anywhere.

I got a job over on the neighboring Menneke Ranch. Ed Menneke's place wasn't as big as the Diamond A—it was only about 120 sections—but he had both sheep and cattle, branded with a triangle on their sides.

I worked with both sheep and cattle while I was there—riding out to visit the Mexican sheepherders and their flocks at their camps, and riding out to the cattle to see if any of their brands were blooming. If flies had gotten into the brands—if they'd bloomed with worms—we'd doctor them with a dope bottle we always carried on our saddles.

This was another bunkhouse situation, but soon after I arrived, I was sent to the north side of the Capitans, where Menneke had a little place close to the Capitan Gap, the big pass that divides the west mountain from the main bulk. I lived in the house there while working on a trough line that needed repair.

At that time, a lot of homesteads and ranches along the Capitan Mountains, both the south side and the north side, were fed by mountain springs. The ranchers and farmers built what they called trough lines from the springs down to their dwellings and corrals. The lines were made of logs up to twenty feet long that had their bark peeled off and troughs cut in them. The first log would be placed at the spring head, that one lapped over onto another one, and so forth down the mountainside, all the way to the house and corrals. The trough lines

*Menneke Ranch, also known as Koprian Ranch,
north side of the Capitans.*

were made of pine, and they didn't last that long because of the action
of the water; they had to be rebuilt once in a while. But Menneke got
the bright idea to run a concrete trough line down the mountain. That
sounded all right, and it was a good trough for a while, but the roots of
the trees along the mountains finally broke up the concrete; it was
always needing repair.

By contrast, the Merchant Ranch, a neighboring ranch where I went
to work later in the summer of 1927, had gum springs up on the west
side of the mountains, and they put in a two-inch pipe that worked
pretty well. Just think of that good, soft, spring water from up in the
mountains coming down into the headquarters, where it would go
through a trough or into a basin and then, overflowing that, down into
a tank where the livestock would drink. That was satisfaction!

While I was still working on the Menneke trough line, I had an
opportunity to rent a cabin just north of Capitan Gap, on the edge of
the timber, with 160 acres and a fenced pasture. It was called the Pater-

son Place because a family named Paterson had filed on it, but they had moved on and lived elsewhere. It was now rented by Old Man Dixon, who lived on the south side of the gap but still ran a few head of cattle in the pasture. The cabin was vacant, so Dixon rented it to me for five dollars a month and a promise to keep the fences in repair and rebuild the corrals.

This would be my home for the next three years.

It was a beautifully made log cabin, with a good, tight tin roof that didn't leak. There was a kitchen range in the lean-to, and a big room for living and sleeping. I fixed it up so that it was nice and comfortable, and soon had a bunch of cats for company and chickens for eggs. Eventually I also bought two more horses—a black named Blackjack and a flax-maned sorrel called Flax.

There was no water on the place, but there was a cistern by the kitchen door where you could get water for household use that came off the tin roof through a pipe. It was good, soft rainwater. My horses and Dixon's cattle watered at a tank, an earthen depression with the sides built up alongside an arroyo; when it rained, the tank would fill up like a lake. In dry times, I had to take my horses over to another place to water them.

I got the idea now that I didn't have to work all year round. In the spring it was calf roundups and shipping on the cattle ranches, and on the sheep ranches it would be lambing in the spring, shearing in the summer, and shipping in the winter. I figured that I could work just so much a year and then settle down in my cabin with enough money to keep me in supplies and take care of all my needs the rest of the year.

It seemed to work. I'd go down at roundup time, and help wrestle calves for branding and castrating for a few days or weeks at two dollars a day. Then I'd ride into Capitan with my pack horse and load up on supplies at Titworth Store, and come back and settle in at the Paterson place.

You could buy a lot for very little back then. I'd buy coffee, flour for making biscuits, bacon, baking powder and baking soda, and beans—pinto beans. Along with a supply of eggs from my chickens, it was practically a continuous breakfast. I very seldom ate meat, but once in a while they would butcher over at a ranch and I would get some beef.

My flax-mane sorrel and I, 1929, north of the Capitan Mountains.

Black Range headquarters.

Whenever I would leave to ride chuck line, neighbors would come in every now and then to throw feed out to the chickens, and the cats took care of themselves, hunting outside. The door was never locked, and oftentimes, when I would come back, I would notice that somebody had been by and cooked a meal for themselves, maybe stayed overnight, and gone on. That was the custom back then. Nothing was ever stolen.

Sometimes I would work for the Mennekes, and sometimes for the Merchants—the brothers, Lon and Roy (or Bug, as he was called), and the old father, Wallace, who used to be a buffalo hunter. The Merchant Ranch was a small one, with only eighty sections; it used the bridle-bit brand—two circles with a bar in between.

Around this time, I was beginning to think that someday I would like to be a writer. I had fallen in love with New Mexico, and wanted to write something about it.

Then, one day while I was living at the Paterson place—in October of 1927—I rode my horse to a sort of a bench on the north side of the Capitans, and I looked below onto the great flatland that extended eastward, down into the Pecos Valley, across the Caprock and the Llano Estacado—the Staked Plains—and into Texas.

There was a road down there, the Spindle Route—two ruts was all it was, really—going 130 miles from Capitan to Roswell. On it, coming my way, were two covered wagons, each pulled by a couple of horses, and a man on horseback driving a small herd of milk cattle. Homesteaders.

I looked down at them, and said to myself, "Here is my West." Those were the people I wanted to write about. I watched as they drove their wagons and cattle up to an abandoned homestead, the King place, and then I rode back home.

A couple days later, I rode down and introduced myself. The families' names were Winkler and Shaw. The Winkler bunch was Paw—the old man—his son, and the son's wife; and the Shaws were Winkler's daughter, her husband, and some little children. They had come all the way from Atoka County in eastern Oklahoma, camping out night after night after night. What impressed me most about them was that right after they got settled in, they went out with plow and implements, broke a field that hadn't been cultivated in several years, and planted it. They were hard-working people.

We had a real neighborly situation. I used to go to their house quite often, and they'd always welcome me—"C'mon in. We're havin' dinner. We got coffee, we got beans."

Once on Christmas I brought what I thought were some special foods that they would like. The canned shrimp didn't work out. "Get those maggots out of here," Paw yelled. "We wouldn't eat those damned things for anything," he said.

Otherwise we got along fine.

The Winklers and Shaws had a bunch of chickens—little banties they had brought all the way from Oklahoma, and egg-laying chickens. And Paw was awfully proud, showing me the gaffs he had for his fighting cocks.

69

These were earthy people—people who lived by what they could get out of the soil—and I liked them for that. I liked them also for their language—their vernacular—which I studied as they told me stories of where they'd come from in eastern Oklahoma, right at the foot of the Kiamichi Mountains in the Ozarks. Their ancestors had been in the Ozarks for generations.

I don't think the Winklers and Shaws ever really bothered to homestead, to claim the land. They just went onto abandoned homesteads as they traveled, and squatted. They were real people of the earth.

In later years, when I was writing for a living, they were the prototypes for my novel *In Time of Harvest*.

I had a lot of other neighbors around the Paterson place, both Spanish and Anglo. The Anglos were mostly homesteaders who had come from other states—Texas, Oklahoma, Arkansas—and had filed on parcels of land along the base of the mountains. They cleared fields off, built cabins, and had their little farms. Then there were the Spanish from the villages of Richardson and Encinosa. The Block Ranch and the Merchant Ranch were also within a few miles, and the Menneke Ranch was further up in the gap in the timber. I worked on all three.

One of my neighbors was Casimiro, a Yaqui Indian from Mexico. He was a real old-timer, and had known Billy the Kid. He looked about fifty-five years old, but Casimiro was at least ninety, and might have been a hundred years old.

He once had a place in Arabela, a village on the east end of the Capitans. That's where he was living when Billy the Kid escaped from the Lincoln County Courthouse in 1881. The Kid first went to Las Tablas, where he got a blacksmith to cut off his leg irons, and then he went to Casimiro's and hid out there while things were hot. When the coast was clear, he took off again. Casimiro advised The Kid to take off for Mexico, but Billy didn't, and of course Pat Garrett eventually caught up with him at Fort Sumner and killed him.

Another neighbor was Old Man Hipp—a good farmer, an excellent farmer—who lived next to the King place. I helped bury him, and that's what gave me the inspiration for *Death in the Claimshack*.

Old Man Hipp got pneumonia. He caught a cold, and it went into pneumonia, and he died. Lon Merchant came over to my place, and

With three friends at the Fuller Ranch, 1930. I am at the right.

Dining area at Bill Kelsey's fencing camp on the sheep hills south of Picacho, Treat Ranch, 1930. Photo by the author, whose shadow blurs a portion of the potrack.

said, "C'mon, Old Man Hipp died. We gotta bury him. Everybody's coming over there to bury him." It was early in the morning—dead winter—and the snow on the ground was about two feet deep and crusted over. I got my horse, saddled up, and rode over to the Hipp place with Lon, our horses going "crunch, crunch, crunch" through the snow all the way. When we got into the shack, the stink of formaldehyde just about knocked us over; somebody had already painted the old man with formaldehyde. They'd sent to Carrizozo for a coffin. In *Death in the Claimshack*, I had them tear down the privy to make the casket.

It was damned hard work digging in that frozen ground, but Lon and I and some of the Block Ranch cowboys went at it with picks and shovels, and after a while we finally got under the frost, and then it wasn't so bad. It was Lloyd Taylor, the foreman of the Block Ranch, that I patterned Mr. Daylor after in the novel.

Later on, I moved to a cabin on the Merchant Ranch—the Red Cabin—and I stayed up there from 1930 to 1933.

There was no water at all at the cabin. I had to take my two pack horses, a keg on each side of them, and fill the kegs at the ranch house, three miles away. Then I'd ride back and pour the water into a barrel I kept for that purpose.

The Merchants were great readers. They only had a few books, but they subscribed to a lot of magazines—*Saturday Evening Post*, *Collier's*, *Cosmopolitan*—and of course *Cosmopolitan* wasn't a women's magazine back then; a lot of good writers used to write for it. I used to borrow magazines from the Merchants and read them at my cabin.

It was at the Red Cabin that I got my first bookshelf. I got a box at Titworth Store in Capitan, and brought it up by pack horse. I nailed it onto the wall,   and used a tomato can as a bookend. I didn't have too many books, but they meant a lot to me—Roark Bradford's *John Henry*, Stuart Chase's *Mexico*, Maurice Fulton and Pat Garrett's *Authentic Life of Billy the Kid*, John A. Lomax's *Cowboy Songs and Other Frontier Ballads*, a couple of Zane Grey Westerns, and a few others.

It was also at the Red Cabin that I began taking notes, deepening my desire to become a writer. But there was still other work to do; it would be some time before I could turn full-time to writing.

*The author at Casey's Ranch,
near Picacho in the Hondo Valley, 1931.*

While I was living there, I started working on sheep ranches down in the Picacho country, in the Hondo Valley at the east end of the Capitans. At that time, Mexican sheepherders still lived in tents while they herded their flocks on the range, but that was becoming a thing of the past. Sheep ranchers were now fencing in the pastures so that the sheep could run loose.

I continued that life—working part-time and returning to live by myself in the Red Cabin—until 1933. Then I met Bill Lumpkins.

Every now and then, Mother Merchant—Lon and Bud Merchant's mother—would give a nice party, a Sunday-school-type party, for all their neighbors and friends from Capitan. There would be games to play, quilting bees, and bible readings. The cowboys came because they were attracted to the food, and I was among them. I wasn't interested in church outings, but I did like the food! Bill and his wife Jeanette used to come out there, and Bill was no more a church person than I was.

Bill was the middle son of William Lumpkins, who had a small ranch in the Vera Cruz Mountains west of the Capitans. Bill had studied in California and at the University of New Mexico in Albuquerque, and was doing some exceptional work as a watercolorist. Later, of course, he would become quite famous.

We got to know each other at one of Mother Merchant's parties, and I told him that I was taking notes and writing; that my ambition was to be a writer, and I was going to follow it through.

The only other person I'd ever told that to was Cap Mossman, one day in 1927 when we were driving into Roswell from the Diamond A. Cap had said, "Go to it, boy. But don't ever let the boys back in the bunkhouse know that, or they'll never have any use for you."

Bill told me, "You're wasting your time here. Why don't you move up to Santa Fe? There's a lot of creative people there—artists and writers. That's where you belong. You don't belong out in this cow pasture."

In June of 1933, Bill and Jeanette took me on my first trip to Santa Fe. We drove in a touring car, and it was quite an adventure for me. There was a hill called Nogal on the road between Capitan and Carrizozo, a hairpin thing—you went straight down, and then you'd

Santa Fe in the Thirties

I was so taken by Santa Fe that later in the year I decided to move up that way with my three horses and my few possessions. I rode all the way on horseback from the north side of the Capitans, about 175 miles in all. I went east of the Jicarilla Mountains, north of Lincoln, until I got to the end of them, turned north over towards Corona, and then from Corona rode up towards the Estancia Valley. There were no paved routes anywhere, so I just followed the dirt road, and it was easy on the horses. My books, my tent, and my sheepherder's stove and cooking utensils had been sent ahead to Santa Fe by mail, so I just carried some clothing, bedding, and a little food with me. I stopped at a couple of ranches on the way, staying overnight and then going on in the morning. One night, I stayed at a sheep camp with some Mexican sheepherders.

I stopped first at the upper end of the Estancia Valley near Galisteo, about fifteen miles south of Santa Fe. Bill Lumpkins had bought five acres of land there, up by Cañoncito in Apache Canyon, a little canyon that goes along the Galisteo River near where it comes down from Glorieta Baldy. Bill and I rolled rocks down from the hillside and laid out a little house with rocks and mud mortar. It was a two-story affair, with one room downstairs and one room upstairs. Bill intended to use it as a guest house after he built a larger dwelling there. He was already an expert at building.

During the next year, I lived in my tent in Apache Canyon in the Sangre de Cristos, at 8,500 feet. That winter was a tough one, with deep snow that piled up around the tent and often made the top and sides sag, but I had plenty of wood to keep me warm. In the summer months, I'd go up to a reservoir on top of Glorieta Mesa to swim, and I could bathe in the river below. My horses grazed up and down the canyon. At night, I would hobble one of them so that they would stay together. It was a good life.

Burros laden with wood coming in to Santa Fe.

Sometimes I'd ride into Santa Fe on Kid and go shopping at Theodore Roybal's store on Galisteo Street, opposite the Old Mexico Store. Roybal's had a big lot in front where the wood-yard workers would bring in loads of wood for sale on the backs of their burros. At Roybal's I would stock up on food—bread, flour, salt, coffee, beans, potatoes, and great slabs of bacon. Then I'd head back the same day—a thirty-mile round- trip.

While I was living in Apache Canyon, I got acquainted with Milt Haymes—an Ozarker, an old mountaineer with a white beard. He lived up on the top of Glorieta Mesa in an old-time log cabin. Milt asked me, "Why don't you come up and stay with me for a while and batch?"

I said, "I sure would like to do that." So I got my three horses together and moved in with him up there on the mesa.

Here I was, back with the Winklers again! Milt was from Arkansas, and he spoke the same language as those Winklers who had inspired me in the Capitans. He had come from Arkansas into Oklahoma, from Oklahoma into the Texas Panhandle, from there into

Tucumcari in eastern New Mexico, and finally to Glorieta Mesa.

Milt's cabin had no water, and it was too deep to drill a well there, so we used to haul water with Milt's team and wagon from Padre Springs, which was nearby.

Sometimes we'd ride the team down to Glorieta, on a very steep grade. There was a road, but it was practically straight down and awful to travel on with a team and a wagon. Every time we went to town we had to cut down a tree and tie it to the back of the wagon with a rope. Then we'd start down the road with the tree holding the wagon like an anchor, and the team would pull that tree and the wagon down the side of the mesa.

All the time I was batching with Milt, I was taking notes on his talk, and it was through him and the homesteaders I had met while living down south that I learned the vernacular I used later in my novels *In Time of Harvest, Death in the Claimshack*, and *Cousin Drewey and the Holy Twister*.

Back to Lincoln County

I knew Santa Fe was where I wanted to ultimately live, but I was running low on money, so in 1936 I got on my horses and went back down to Lincoln County to work on the ranches. But instead of going up the north side of the Capitans, this time I went down into the sheep country south of the Hondo River and around Picacho. There, I worked the ranches for another year, the sheep ranches particularly, as they had more work than the cattle ranches at that time. And I liked sheep—especially when they were running loose in the pastures.

I worked quite a bit for Bill Kelsey, a wonderful old cowboy who was building fences for sheep ranches. Bill could do anything; he was an irrigation farmer, a dry-land farmer, a chuck-wagon cook, and a master at sourdough bread.

It was during this time that I wrote my first article, a little one-pager called "Meals—25¢." I wrote it out longhand and sent it off to *West*, a pulp Western magazine. The article was about a Block Ranch foreman named Tom Pridemore, who was mean as hell. Of course, I didn't use his real name.

Pridemore had a steep hill by headquarters, and when cowboys would come by and ask him for a job, he'd say, "All right, let's see how you can manage a horse." They'd have to ride up to the top of the hill, and then ride right down the side of it. There are two graves at the bottom of the hill that are supposed to be where two cowboys are buried who failed Pridemore's entry examination. That's how mean Pridemore was.

"Meals—25¢" is about two cowboys who came by riding chuck line, wanting a meal and a place to stay overnight in exchange for work. Pridemore let them stay, all right, but in the morning he charged them twenty-five cents a meal. That was a great disgrace in those days, when hospitality was the rule. After those cowboys left, they came in among some Block cattle, roped a big calf, tied it down, got their running irons out, and—right under the big Block brand—branded that calf, "Meals—25¢."

West paid me a dollar for the story.

By the end of the winter of 1936–37, I was ready to move back to Santa Fe. I was working on the Fuller Ranch, run by Pen Fuller. I liked it there because Pen had a very good study, with a desk, typewriter, and shelves and shelves of books that I could just help myself to. He had a good selection of southwestern books. The first time I saw *Death Comes for the Archbishop* was there, when Mrs. Fuller pulled it off the shelf and showed it to me.

One day Pen asked me, "You're not a cook, are you?"

I said, "Hell, I've been cooking for myself for a long time, feeding myself."

"Mrs. Fuller is going to go east for a while. Would you come and do the cooking at the ranch? The boys would like your kind of cooking."

"Well, sure, I suppose I could do that. I was going to head up to Santa Fe, but I'll stick around a while and cook for you, sure."

As the new cook, my day started before light with cooking breakfast for Pen and three or four other men. It was cow-camp cooking—beans, fried potatoes, fried eggs, fried salt pork, and once in a while lamb or beefsteak. It wasn't anything fancy, but the men liked my cooking fine—and old Pen himself took it too. What they especially liked, though, was my German potato bread.

While I was in Apache Canyon, I had gotten acquainted with an

Milt Haynes, the Ozarker, at Glorieta Mesa, 1934.

artist there named Helmuth Naumer. He lived down from my camp, and I used to go out to his place a lot. He and his wife were German, and I used to go over there because he was always interested in hearing me tell about life on the ranches down in the cow country. His wife was a wonderful cook, and she used to make a German potato bread. I loved that potato bread so much that I asked her how she made it. When I got to the Fuller Ranch, I got that recipe out and started in on it— and it came out perfect! So I made big loaves of potato bread—hard-crusted and hot inside when it came out fresh from the oven—and the fellows liked it because it was a change from the eternal biscuit. Pen Fuller liked it, too.

While I was cooking there, I had a lot of time for either reading Pen's books or just sitting around doing nothing, and one day I thought, "Here's where I'm going to write!"

I borrowed Pen's typewriter, and even though I could only hunt-and-peck on it, I wrote an article about the sheep ranches and wolf-proof fencing. I kept it stored away for a couple of months—didn't do anything with it at all. And then I thought, "The state has a magazine. Why not send it to the state magazine?" So I put the article in an envelope and sent it to *New Mexico Magazine*. George Fitzpatrick was the editor then, and damned if I didn't soon get a letter from him saying that my article, "Shepherds on Horseback," was accepted. It was published in the September 1937 issue of *New Mexico Magazine*. I was paid thirteen dollars and fifty cents. Boy, was that big money in those days!

I said to myself, "Here I am, a writer, now—Santa Fe bound."

A New Life

The cowboy life for me was no more. Once again, I rode up to Santa Fe, with my three horses and two others I had bought from Add Casey at the McKnight Ranch. When I got to Santa Fe, I sold them to Tex Austin, a big, blustery rodeo promoter who was running the Forked Lightning Ranch in Pecos as a dude ranch. Greer Garson has it now. They were good, gentle horses, just right for dudes.

Austin was quite a character. Later he opened up a restaurant on the plaza in Santa Fe. His specialty was oysters on the half shell. What people didn't know was that Tex had a collection of oyster shells that he used to wash over and over again with the dishes. Tex would buy canned oysters and use ice to get them real cold; put the canned oysters on the shells; add a slice of lemon; and that was Tex's great delicacy, oysters on the half shell. Nobody seemed to know the difference.

It hurt me to sell my horses, but I knew cowboying was over for me. I wanted to write. Incidentally, that was the last time I rode a

Fuller Ranch, 1937.

horse, because I believe thoroughly that you don't ride a horse for pleasure; you ride a horse for either transportation or work. My horses had served me well, and they were going into a pretty good life when I sold them to Tex.

At that time, there was an Englishman named Rupert Samuelson who had a place fifteen miles from Santa Fe, just down from where I had camped in Apache Canyon. He was always building an adobe house somewhere, and I went over there and helped him on this one. I was the only Anglo working for him; the others were Mexicans. Samuelson was of the English nobility and was so polite. My job was to pick up the fresh adobes and take them over to Rupert, who was putting them in place. Every time I'd give him an adobe, he said, "Oh, thank you, Johnny!" I stayed on for a while with Samuelson, but I soon got bored. It was all right, but there was no future there. It wasn't my kind of life.

While I was living in Santa Fe, I got to know a woman named Helen Cunningham, who knew all the artists and writers there.

She asked me one day, "Say, are you looking for work that would suit your writing?"

I said, "Certainly!"

"There's a job open over at the Palace of the Governors, at the Museum of New Mexico, as a research assistant on their extension projects."

I asked her what kind of work it would be, and she said, "Mostly writing articles and papers on exhibits that are going to be put up in the branch museums, and doing research and writing for the Extension Service."

I went over to the Governor's Palace and saw Ina Sizer Cassidy, who was in charge of the Museum Extension Service. I told her I was interested in the job, and she decided to give me a try. She put me on there at fifty dollars a month! Ina was the widow of Gerald Cassidy, the famous Santa Fe artist. She and I later became very good friends.

They wanted some good publicity about projects they were working on. Ina said, "We want you to write some newspaper articles for the *Santa Fe New Mexican* on what we're doing here." They were organizing quite a few branch museums throughout New Mexico—in Carlsbad, Raton, Portales, Las Vegas, Silver City, Lincoln, and other places. I would do research and then write a paper for the construction of dioramas. One project in Clovis was on paleontology because of the Blackwater Draw lake bed and the discoveries there of mammoths and paleo-Indian artifacts. In Lincoln, it was the escape of Billy the Kid. In Silver City, it was on mining.

One of my projects was an ethnobotany exhibit that was to go into all the branch museums, and I had to go all over Santa Fe and interview old Mexican women—*curanderas*—who used these natural medicines. God, it was fascinating! They put an example of each herb or plant in a glass-covered box, and on the back they described the plant and how and what it was used for in medicine. There must have been hundreds of these boxes. That exhibit went around to all the branch museums. I don't know if it still exists or not. I know there were still some of those frames at the Coronado State Monument when I was there later.

While I was researching and writing for the Extension Service, I had a typewriter and worked in a room in the back patio of the Palace

The plaza in Santa Fe.

of the Governors. At that time, there was a literary magazine starting up called the *Santa Fe Sentinel,* and I started writing articles for it. There was also another one called the *Santa Fe Examiner,* and I started writing articles for that one, too.

Sometimes the editors asked me to write a particular piece, and sometimes I queried them and asked them what they would be interested in. Margaret Loeker, who later went to Dallas, where she became the editor of the *Southwest Review,* was the editor of the *Santa Fe Examiner.* She published everything I wrote! I continued writing for *New Mexico Magazine* also. After the September 1937 issue, I had another piece in the December issue—"Vaquero Lingo"—and from then on it was steady work for *New Mexico Magazine.* During this time I was

A street in Santa Fe.

writing a lot of cowboy stuff for local newspapers and magazines, too. I also wrote the first draft of *Death in the Claimshack* while working for the Extension Service; it was to be published by Caxton, but then the war came along, and they didn't publish it.

The new job enabled me to rent a place on Upper Canyon Road from Beatriz Vigil, in that little section called Los Vigiles where Canyon Road comes onto Camino del Monte Sol. The Vigil family owned a lot of houses around there that they rented out. Mine was a little house between Canyon Road and the Acequia Madre. I paid ten dollars a month rent, and had a lot of money left for food. The house didn't have any water in it, so I had to go to a faucet at the side of Beatriz Vigil's house and fill up a bucket; that was my water supply. But there was electricity, so I bought a King heater, a little wood heater. You could cook on the top of it and heat the house at the same time.

I had to get wood, so I'd borrow a wheelbarrow from Beatriz Vigil and go down to Rios's wood yard and fill it up for twenty-five cents. Jesús Rios's wood yard was at the corner of Camino del Monte Sol and Canyon Road. Everyone got their wood from Jesús back then, and his family is still operating the business. Then I'd push that wheelbarrow all the way back up to my little house. In the wintertime, the snow might sometimes be eighteen inches high, but if I was out of wood, I had to do it anyway. That's how I warmed my place. Of course, even in the summertime I had to get wood, because that's all I had to cook on—that little woodstove.

I'd go to Roybal's for my groceries; he had a good selection of fresh vegetables. The Safeway stores were also there then, and another store called Batrite. If you wanted real luxury, though, you went to Kaune's, a super-luxury grocery store; everything they had was exceptionally good, especially their meats and bread

Artists and Writers

Canyon Road was wonderful in those days! It was unpaved, with beautiful cottonwoods and the mountains looming right ahead of you, and it was home to many of Santa Fe's best artists and writers—Olive Rush, Randall Davey, Odon Hullenkremer, and others. The area seemed very, very primitive. And that air—that Santa Fe air was something!

The artists who came in and settled along Canyon Road—if they had to build a house, it was the old one-story adobe. That was the typical house, and the patios were very lovely. You'd step off the road through a gate into a little patio, and on one side were the living quarters, and on the other side were the outside buildings, all along the patio. It was very delightful.

All the artists living up on Canyon Road followed that pattern—all but Georgio Belloli. He built a house in the Venetian style, all out of kilter with the others. It was a beautiful house, but it didn't belong on Canyon Road in Santa Fe. He later became famous for the Santa Fe style of architecture, though, and in his later years he went to Mexico, to Guanajuato, and restored a lot of the old colonial buildings down there.

I was included in the artists' circle. I knew all of them—Randall Davey and Datus Myers, Will Shuster and Sheldon Parsons, Odon Hullenkremer and Alfred Morang.

Odon Hullenkremer was Hungarian, a nice old fellow, and he talked like a Hungarian. He had a studio on Las Piedras, by my place, and we used to talk on his front porch and watch the traffic go by. I walked down his street one day in midwinter, right after a snowstorm. The snow had melted during the day, and there were long, thick icicles coming down from the canales on Odon's roof. I stopped to talk, and he said to me, "I remember one time there was a man. He walked down the street. He came to one of those icicles, and he gave it a swat. And it hit him on the head and killed him, *incidentally!*"

There's a lot of his paintings in La Fonda, right by the information desk.

Alfred Morang was famous for his parties up there off the acequia in Placita Rafaela. He had a beautiful house that only cost him twenty-five dollars a month. I thought his was very expensive at twenty-five dollars because I was only paying ten dollars a month for mine. Those parties that he had were terrific, and all the artists went to them. He was the picture of Bohemia.

I remember one night at a party of Alfred's the poet Witter Bynner came by. We called him Hal. He and I were talking, and then this girl came up to me. She was a Guatemalan artist or collector, and was living in Santa Fe. She'd seen me there, sitting next to Bynner, and she came over and said, "Oh, you're John Sinclair."

I said, "Yes."

And she said, "They tell me how popular you are in Santa Fe."

I asked, "Who told you that?"

"Oh, everybody." But then she said, "I'm terribly disappointed, now that I've met you."

I said, "Oh, is that so?"

She said, "They said you were handsome. You're not handsome."

I said, "No, I know that."

I think Hal was talking to somebody else at that time while she was going on like this, and I don't know if he'd heard the girl telling me how

Adobe factory in Santa Fe.

disappointed she was with me; he may have. But finally she went off, and Hal and I got to talking again.

Then after a while, she came back over. She wasn't interested in me anymore; she wanted to talk to Bynner.

"So you're the famous Witter Bynner, are you?"

"Yes. . . ," he said. ". . .You know, I think you're very attractive."

She replied, "Oh, I'm so glad."

And then he went on, with all his great poetic skill, to describe her beauty, and she was in rapture. Bynner described her eyes, her mouth, her hair, her wonderful complexion—she had a little bit of Maya in her. Bynner told her that he could tell by her words that she was intelligent, that she was brilliant; she was so beautiful, so desirable, so intelligent. Everything that the poet had in him came out in his description of her, and she was completely taken over. He praised her to the skies.

Here was the famous poet Witter Bynner telling her how beautiful she was, how desirable, how intelligent, and on and on and on.

Then finally he looked in her eyes, and he said to her, ". . . and out of your ass drops shit!"

She sputtered, said she would never come back to another party in Santa Fe, and went out the door.

Alfred was a great friend of Erskine Caldwell, the author of *Tobacco Road* and *God's Little Acre*. Caldwell used to come to Santa Fe quite often. Alfred was always broke, and Erskine paid his rent.

When Alfred Morang was back in Boston, he used to go to these dives in Boston and paint the prostitutes and the drunks, and in Santa Fe he did the same thing. He did this one watercolor painting of a woman lying on a couch with nothing on. Oh gosh, I remember when I bought that painting. I gave three dollars for it.

I showed the painting to several people, and one woman said, "There's something wrong with that." She said, "This woman has breasts, but she doesn't have any nipples."

And I said, "Gosh, maybe we can get that remedied."

So I took the painting over to Alfred's and said to him, "Alfred, look at this. Everyone says that this woman doesn't have any nipples on her breasts." I said to him, "Put a little dab of pink there, Alfred, and she'll be all right."

Alfred stared at me. He said, "Do you know what mixture it takes on the palette to make nipples? Pink? No, you have to get this and you have to get that, and this and that, and then you have to mix it together, and then—*only* then—have you got nipples." But he got out his palette and he started mixing up his paints, and then with his brush he went, "pook! pook!"

And she had nipples.

There was another thing I liked about living up on Canyon Road. At the end of Canyon Road, there was always La Fonda Hotel! In the wintertime it was very cold, and there was lots of snow, but we enjoyed it. We'd wade in the snow all the way down to La Fonda, and we'd go into the cantina there and have coffee or whatever.

The writers and artists used to meet regularly in the cantina. If you went in at the cocktail hour, they would all be sitting around drinking and talking; it was a very social atmosphere. There were other hotels—the Montezuma and the De Vargas, and such—but they were nothing like La Fonda. At the restaurant over there, they had a chef named Conrad who had once been chef to the Kaiser of Germany. We used to go into the cantina at La Fonda for breakfast or lunch, and for sixty-five cents we'd get some of the most wonderful food. Eggs Benedict was the famous La Fonda breakfast. Bee Bee Dunne introduced me to that.

Bee Bee Dunne

I was a great friend of Bee Bee Dunne, who was quite a town character at that time. He was a dried-guy who wore a big hat, a great fur coat, and jodhpur trousers—not men's jodhpurs, but women's. Every time Bee Bee took a leak he had to pull down his whole damned pants; you'd see him in the men's room of La Fonda, standing over a urinal, and he'd have his trousers all pulled down because they didn't have a fly.

He was retired from the *Santa Fe New Mexican*, where he had started in 1910 as a reporter, going around Santa Fe on horseback to get his stories. He also used to sit around La Fonda with a little black book and a pen, interviewing people who came into the hotel—not so much ordinary tourists, but people who were well known.

Then he got into other things. He built a house up on the corner of the Acequia Madre and East Garcia streets, just where the Acequia Madre ended and where Manhattan Street started. It was a low adobe house with thick walls—typical Santa Fe style, where you had to walk through huge double gates into a patio before you could get into the house. Bee Bee had a wonderful door in his house. He had an enlarged, life-size photograph of the Venus de Milo, and when he built his house, he had the builders put this cut-out of the Venus de Milo against the wall; and they had to make a door no wider than that photograph and no higher. Bee Bee said that no woman could go through that door unless she had the figure of the Venus de Milo! That was the way Bee Bee was his whole life. He was a character!

Bee Bee was drinking a lot when I first went to Santa Fe. The first time I met him was about 1934. I was living up on Glorieta Mesa, and would come down into Santa Fe and go over to La Fonda. I had just come off the ranches, and I was a typical working cowboy; I dressed like a cowboy, and I looked like a cowboy.

I was sitting in a chair at La Fonda one day, and Bee Bee came up and sat by me.

"You know what they did in the cantina?" he asked me.

"What?"

He said, "They put me out of the cantina and told me not to go in there. So, I'll tell you what to do. You go in there, into the cantina, and buy me a bottle of champagne." That's all he ever drank in those days, and he'd get terribly drunk.

I said, "I think you've had enough."

So he said, "Well, I'll make a trade with you. I can see that you're interested in horses."

I said, "Yes, I am. I've been interested in horses for a long time."

"Well," he said, "you don't know it, but I'm the world's foremost authority on horses. If you'll buy me a bottle of champagne from the cantina—and I'll give you the money for it—you come back here, and I'll tell you things about horses that you don't know."

I said, "Sir, I'm sorry. I think you've had enough champagne."

He said, "Well, all right, if that's the way you feel. If you don't want to learn about horses, I'll just leave you."

And he got up and walked off.

He came back a little while later. He had gone to his house and gotten an Indian blanket and a lot of Indian jewelry—he had the most wonderful collection of Indian jewelry you ever saw; in fact, he had baskets full of all kinds of beautiful Indian jewelry—squash-blossom necklaces, concho belts, everything. He came back to La Fonda wearing the blanket and carrying some silver jewelry on a string. Fordham, the house detective, was sitting on a bench and watching—he had been told to keep Bee Bee out of the cantina—and here comes this Indian with a blanket over his head. He went up to Fordham and, of course, Fordham didn't even recognize him, and so Bee Bee got into the cantina.

That was life at La Fonda. Incidentally, you could get a good room there for about a dollar and a half.

There's quite a story behind how Bee Bee finally quit drinking. He was at La Fonda as usual, and had ordered his champagne from a barmaid known as La Lulu. She was really quite famous.

La Lulu took Bee Bee's order, and then looked at him, and he looked at her.

"I'm sorry that I'm not going to be seeing you much longer," she told him, "because you're going to die, and soon. You drink too much."

Bee Bee told me that the way she looked at him affected him so much that he never touched liquor again after that; he knew that he was at the end of the line.

Old-timers in front of the Lincoln County Courthouse, 1940.

The Lincoln Museum

Because of my knowledge of Lincoln County, the Museum of New Mexico transferred me to Lincoln in 1940 to establish the Lincoln Museum in the old courthouse, that house of horrors where Billy the Kid made his escape during the Lincoln County War. The Museum of New Mexico had acquired the Lincoln County Courthouse in 1938 and put an archaeologist, J. W. Hendron, in charge of the place. He took the old courthouse when it was about ready to fall to pieces and by 1940 had restored it. That's when I took over. When I moved in—and it was absolutely empty—there was nothing except for white walls, and everything was fresh and clean.

The people in and around Lincoln were very cooperative, although at first there were some of them—the Spanish, particularly—who thought that somebody from Lincoln should have had the job of curator. But there was nobody with that kind of experience in Lincoln.

The courthouse had originally been a store operated by the Murphy and Dolan Company. They were put out of business by the Lincoln County War in 1878, and the building was turned into a county courthouse in 1881. Just inside the entrance was a large room where Murphy and Dolan had operated their store. We installed exhibits of frontier items in that room. On the east side of the building was a room that had been the store's business office, and it became my office and living quarters. The kitchen was in the storeroom, but there was no plumbing there. For water I'd go to a cistern across the street on the La Paloma Bar premises.

The post office of Lincoln was down the street in the old Tunstall-McSween store, which was then being run by Ed Penfield and his family. That was the only store in Lincoln.

My job was to set up the museum and get the place open for the public. All the artifacts were requisitioned, and the display cases came down in trucks from Santa Fe. Then I had to set up the exhibits. Penfield had some things from the Lincoln County War days, and I filled a lot of cases with them. The diorama on Billy the Kid was the big thing. Even during wartime, the story of Billy the Kid would keep tourists coming in.

I had to do a lot of research. I bought books on Lincoln and the Lincoln County War, and Bee Bee Dunne sent me a thirty-nine volume set of Bancroft's works while I was there. The trunk that he sent also contained some wonderful books on nature—reptiles, fauna, trees, and so on.

People still talked about Billy the Kid in Lincoln, of course, and some had known him, but I also did a lot of reading—and, in those earlier years, we had to take what we knew about the Lincoln County War and Billy the Kid, which wasn't much. He may have killed Indians, and he may have killed Spanish; but at the time, the only ones we knew he'd killed were the sheriff, his deputy, and the guards—Brady, Hindman, Bell, and Olinger.

I thought that the first really authentic book on Billy the Kid and the Lincoln County War was done by Frazier Hunt back in the 1950s. Frazier Hunt came to me before the book was published. He had gone to Santa Fe first, and in Santa Fe they advised him to come and see me at the Coronado State Monument—that I could tell him something about Billy the Kid and the Lincoln County War. We talked quite a bit about it.

The name of the book was *The Tragic Days of Billy the Kid*. Frazier—they called him "Spike"—had done a lot of terrific research in the state archives. For instance, he found the marriage license of Billy the Kid's mother when she married in Santa Fe.

There was a strange feeling in that courthouse. It was as spooky as could be! You felt creatures around you—you felt it in the air. I lived in the courthouse right under the window where Billy the Kid shot Olinger. There was an upper balcony outside, and steps going up on either side of the building. I would take tourists up the stairway inside, where Billy shot Bell, and then to the window upstairs where Billy shot Olinger in the street below.

Sometimes, in the middle of the night, I'd hear sounds from up above, from the end of the balcony. I didn't have any electricity—the

Edward Penfield's Store, Lincoln, 1940.

Exhibit room in the Lincoln County Courthouse, 1940.

Old-timer in Lincoln, 1940.

only lighting I had was a Coleman lamp and a stable lamp. So I would pick up the stable lamp and start upstairs, climbing those steps where Billy had shot his guard, Bell. You could sometimes feel them when you were going up those steps—and you had better step over the body! Of course, there was never anything up there, but all the same, you had to keep watch in case a burglar or someone climbed up onto the balcony trying to get in.

I lived in the Lincoln Museum for two and one-half years, and it was there, in 1942, that I wrote my first published novel, *In Time of Harvest*, about a family of pinto-bean farmers struggling to make a living homesteading on New Mexico's central plains. It took me five and one-half months to write it, in longhand; then I typed it out on an Underwood and sent it off to Macmillan. It was published in 1943.

During my tenure at the museum, World War II broke out. I remember the day war was declared. Everybody was feeling so sad, I don't think anybody talked about it for a while. I was called up in the draft, but when I went to Carrizozo for the examination, they declared me 4-F. I thanked God they did. My service at the courthouse wasn't interrupted, and neither was my life. Others weren't so lucky.

I enjoyed working at the old courthouse—enjoyed being a curator; but I hadn't wanted to stay too long. Two and one-half years was just right.

The author, 1943.

Coronado State Monument

I left Lincoln and the museum in 1942 to spend the winter down in Tucson and get the draft of *In Time of Harvest* together.

I went to Tucson because I had a friend there, Nelson Nye, a well-known western writer I'd met when I lived in Santa Fe. He had asked me while I was at Lincoln if I wanted to buy five acres of land close to him, outside of Tucson. The man who owned the land wanted to sell it so he could go back to Florida. The place had a little house on it, a one-room house made of tile—a very bad building material—but the land had a good well on it and lots of water. The place wasn't fenced, but it had all the prospects of being nice once it was fixed up. I got the place for fifteen hundred dollars. I didn't have fifteen hundred to my name, but I got it by paying about ten dollars a month.

Santa Fe was still in me, however, so when spring came, I went back and rented that little house up on Canyon Road again. I went back to the same job with the museum that I'd had before—until May of 1944. That's when the museum asked me if I would take over the Coronado State Monument.

The ruins at the Coronado State Monument are what anthropologists know today as the ancient Tiguex village of Kuaua, a very important historic site because the great explorer Francisco Vásquez Coronado may have established his headquarters there from 1540 to 1542. He and his forces were looking for the fabled Seven Cities of Gold, searching as far east as Kansas and as far west as the Grand Canyon of Arizona. The expedition, of course, was considered by the Spanish to be a failure.

In Coronado's day, Kuaua was a massive dwelling, with two main plazas, six kivas, and a population of about twelve hundred people. And it had one of the most wonderful vistas in the whole state! The village lay about a mile west of the Rio Grande, with the tall grasslands of the valley sweeping northward and southward, crowned by mesas on the

Aerial view of the Kuaua ruins at Coronado State Monument,
the Rio Grande to the East.
Photo courtesy New Mexico Department of Development.

northern and western skylines, and with the giant mass of the Sandia Mountains looming to the east. On the alluvial plain between the village and the river, the villagers had irrigated fields growing corn, squash, cotton, and tobacco. The river has since channeled its waters a mile or so westward, so that Coronado State Monument is now situated just above the river.

In the mid-1930s, the state established Coronado State Park and set aside the ruins of the pueblo as Coronado State Monument; in the hopes that the exact location of Coronado's camp could be determined, the Museum of New Mexico and the University of New Mexico began the work of excavation and restoration. By 1940 it was ready for the Coronado cuartocentennial celebration.

I was in charge of the monument for eighteen years. I arrived with my furniture, my books, typewriter and paper, and a dog and three

Aerial view of Kuaua ruins looking west, 1945.
Photo courtesy New Mexico State Tourist Bureau.

cats. I found the place in shambles. In between custodians, the monument had been vandalized; exhibits had been stolen from the museum. The house that I was to live in had been broken into; the hot-water heater, the kitchen stove, and the bathroom fixtures had all been removed; and there were beer and wine bottles in the fireplace in the living room.

I began the work of getting the entire monument in order again. I hired a Spanish man from Bernalillo, Tranquilino Baca, to help do some of the renovating. He was a real handyman; he could do anything. I also employed Indians from Santa Ana Pueblo—sometimes several generations of a family would come to help with the work—and all together we put the monument back in shape. I liked the Indians very much, and I tried to hire them whenever I could. Time had changed things by the time I took the Coronado job. The cowboy days were a thing of the past for me—even the homesteaders. My attention was now focused on the Indians.

After we got the monument going—got the displays up and the place open to the public—I suggested to the Zia Pueblo women that they come down on Sundays and set up on the portal of the museum; there they could display and sell their pottery. The idea took hold, and entire families would come down and display their crafts on the portal, selling beautiful Zia pottery. Among the items they made were little ashtrays and pots, and sometimes an Indian woman would come up to me with a pot about the size of my palm and say, "This is for you."

Albuquerque was the nearest big town, and the majority of the people who came out to the monument were from there.

I was never entranced with Albuquerque. I could have been, maybe twenty years earlier, right after World War I. I liked the town, all right. It was still a simple place when I was at the monument—a tortilla flat with about forty thousand people—but it isn't today. Today it's Muncie, Indiana. It's an Indiana town for the people who came from Indiana; it's an Ohio town for the people who are coming here from Ohio; and they only see where they came from. They don't see Albuquerque as a New Mexico town. They don't see the Indian pueblos around. They want to make Albuquerque a town in which they can be comfortable—and they'll be comfortable only in an Indiana town or in an Ohio town.

Back then, Albuquerque was still typically New Mexican. You would see Indians on the streets, and it had its Spanish sections where you'd hear only Spanish spoken. Look what it is today—houses up in the heights and all the way to the mountains. They were herding sheep up there when I first came to Albuquerque, and Kirtland Field and Sandia Base were outside the town.

I had very little to do with Albuquerque, going in only for supplies and such. Santa Fe was my town. My employers and my friends were in Santa Fe, not Albuquerque.

Bernalillo, now—that was quite different from Albuquerque.

Our Lady of Sorrows Church, Bernalillo.

Bernalillo was a small, Spanish-and-Indian, dirt-road town. The politics were horrible; it was so crooked that I finally quit voting there. A Spanish *patrón* was in power then, in 1944, and the same families are in power today.

Quite a few Bernalillo townspeople were employed at the lumber mill, where they milled lumber that was brought down from the Jemez Mountains; it was just off the main street. On the main block was the Bernalillo Mercantile, in those days the center of the town.

That main block was everything in Bernalillo. On it were two drugstores. One was on the east side of the street right next to the Bernalillo Mercantile, and it was run by a Syrian and his Spanish wife—Tony and Becky Ziede, a very fine couple. On the other side of the street was a drugstore run by Joe Lovato. He's still living there in Bernalillo, though he sold out a long time ago to a man named Silva, another Syrian with a Spanish wife. I never saw much of the Silvas when I went to town; today they're quite prominent in Bernalillo. Then there was the old church down along the street, built in the 1850s. It's a beautiful little church, restored now after nearly falling to pieces.

I had no car at that time, but I used to enjoy the walk from the monument into Bernalillo—going to the Mercantile, buying a sackful of groceries, and starting home with it. After a while, when the Museum of New Mexico in Santa Fe gave me vehicles to use at the monument, it certainly made shopping easier.

They provided me first with a little panel-body and then with a pickup truck. I'd actually purchased my first car in 1925, just before I went to work for the Diamond A. I didn't purchase my next car, a Chevrolet truck, until I left Coronado State Monument in 1963.

A Break in Superintendency

I had a break in my superintendency from 1945 to 1946. I'd sold a story to the *Saturday Evening Post* and had some money, and decided to go down to Mexico. But for the first part of the break, in the summer, I did some travel writing for *Holiday Magazine*. I went all over New Mexico, Colorado, Utah, and up to Cheyenne, Wyoming.

I traveled with George Thompson, a wonderful photographer. He was working for Sandia Laboratories at that time, but he took off for a while and worked with me, taking pictures with a Speed Graphic. We went up to Navajo country, up around the Four Corners and Monument Valley; and at the St. Christopher Mission in Bluff, Utah, I watched a Navajo lady weaving a rug so beautiful that I wanted to buy it. Reverend Liebler—he was a high-church Episcopalian, very Anglican—was in charge of the mission then. I asked him about the rug, and he told me the cost was twelve dollars. George photographed the woman at her loom, and later when she'd finished, the Reverend Liebler sent it to me.

In the fall, I decided it was time to get down into Mexico. I wanted to finish the final draft of *Death in the Claimshack* there, in a quiet place away from the usual surroundings. I chose Lake Chapala, the largest lake in Mexico, situated about forty miles southeast of Guadalajara, with a little Indian village nearby.

Lake Chapala was immense—forty miles long and twenty miles wide—but not a pretty lake, except for tules on the edges. The water was a sort of dirty yellow. There was a pebbly beach, and Indian women would go down to it and do their laundry, washing clothes in the lake, pounding and wringing them out on metates, and spreading the clothes out on the beach to dry.

The Indians had reed fishing boats, and there were also big sailing vessels that hauled freight back and forth from Chapala, the end of the bus line, to one of the several other towns on the lake. The Indian sailors on the freighters dressed like pirates, with bandanas around their foreheads, earrings hanging from their ears, and big, bloomy trousers like pajamas tied around their waists with sashes. Their feet were bare.

I stayed in a very primitive hut, a pension run by a couple of Germans, that cost me only thirty American dollars a month for room and board. The food was wonderful. They bought white fish caught in the lake, and fruits and vegetables from peddlers.

Some of the food was a little unusual.

In Guadalajara, there was a famous restaurant called La Copa de Leche, Cup of Milk. They had some good food; everybody liked to go there. Most of the menu was in Spanish, and I sometimes didn't know what I was ordering.

One time I ordered something called *ciruelos*. Gosh, it was good—beautiful slices of meat covered with delicious sauce and gravy. After a while I got to wondering at what I was enjoying so much, and I called the waitress over and asked her what it was.

"*Testicles de toro*," she said. Bull testicles.

But I kept on eating. Boy, they were good.

Evelyn

When I finished writing *Death in the Claimshack*, I returned to Coronado State Monument in the spring of 1947, and it was then that I married Evelyn.

I had met Evelyn in 1939 at the Plaza Cafe, which was owned by a Greek family and had the best cream of chicken soup that you could ever eat. I was sitting in a booth there with a fellow named Val Ward when she came in and sat at another booth.

Val said, "Hey, have you ever met Foxy?"

I said, "Who's Foxy?"

"Oh, she's up there at the anthropology lab. You ought to see Foxy. She's good-lookin'."

"Yeah?"

"Oh, sure."

Val went over to her, said, "Hello, Foxy," and introduced me.

Oh, she was good-looking. She was beautiful. We talked for a while, and then I said, "Well, I'll see you sometime," and she said, "Yes."

Late on an evening sometime later, Val and I had a cantaloupe with us, and Val said, "Let's go wake up Foxy." Her maiden name was Fox. Evelyn was boarding at a house up by Fort Marcy Park. So we went up there and got Evelyn—it turned out she wasn't asleep—and the three of us came back down to the plaza and ate that cantaloupe, sitting by the statue in the center of the plaza.

At that time, Evelyn was at the Laboratory of Anthropology, working on Indian designs. She'd already been to Yale, where she had worked for a long time on the Peabody collection of Indian designs. Later, after I met her, she worked with the University of Illinois as a researcher for Rexford Newcombe, the dean of the art department. She had gone to schools in Gainesville, Texas, and got a degree in art education at the Texas State College for Women at Denton. Evelyn was a talented artist. Her mother's people were French-Canadians, and she had spent a lot of her time in Canada when she was younger.

In 1940 the museum sent me to Lincoln, and then in 1944 I went to the Coronado State Monument, so I didn't see anything of Evelyn for a while. Finally, I did something—I can't remember what it was—and they wrote me up in the museum's publication, *El Palacio*. Evelyn read that where she was working at the time, at the University of Illinois; she wrote to me in Lincoln, and I wrote back. After that we corresponded all the time.

We were married in Santa Fe on Saturday, May 9, 1947. We got Bee Bee Dunne to help us find someone to marry us. He was coming down from Sena Plaza with two girls. He'd been at Villagrá Book Shop. He said to the girls, "Excuse me, I've got to see these two people about a contract." The three of us went looking for a justice of the peace, but we couldn't find any; so Bee Bee said, "We'll go down to the police station and see if the police judge will marry you." I think the judge's

Evelyn Fox, 1944.

name was Sanchez. And the judge said, "Of course, I'll marry you." It was a very simple ceremony.

Evelyn was in her early forties and in the prime of health when we married, and so was I. Evelyn had lost one arm when she was just five years old. She had been playing on a picket fence when she fell and broke her arm. The doctor set the bone, but blood poisoning set in, and the arm had to be amputated. But what she could do with that one arm! You ought to see her separate an egg! And she was strong! We used to walk from the monument to Bernalillo to get groceries—three miles there and three miles back—Evelyn with her one arm carrying a sack of groceries and me with my two arms carrying a sack of groceries all the way from Bernalillo back to the monument.

A display of Zia pottery on the portal, 1948.

Visitors at the Monument

Every day when the monument was open, it was my duty to show the tourists around and explain everything to them, and I would end it all with a trip into the Painted Kiva, where I did most of my talking. The visitors were free before and after that to go into the museum to look at the various exhibits. Evelyn helped me out tremendously by taking tourists around sometimes. That gave me a chance to write—and I was doing a lot of writing then.

Sometimes I would dread the tourists coming in. I used to especially dread school kids. They weren't interested in the Indians at all; it was just the outing that they liked. The kids would immediately start looking for arrowheads and potsherds, and they weren't supposed to do that. Then little horned toads would come by, and they'd catch them and kill them. Some of the most objectionable young people that ever visited the monument were the Boy Scouts.

We had the typical visitors from Albuquerque—probably they'd come originally from the East—who had lived in Albuquerque maybe three or four years before ever seeing the Coronado State Monument or even going out to look at New Mexico. But we had some that it was a joy to take around—families with children, or people coming in pairs. Most of the adults were wonderful.

The first celebrity I had at the monument was Earl Warren, the governor of California at that time. He came into the house and sat down, and we talked for a while.

Another was Ludavic Kennedy from Scotland, and his wife, Moira Shearer, who was a famous ballerina, and the star of *The Red Shoes*. I told them that I had lived at Drumlanrig Castle, and Ludavic said, "Well, that's a coincidence, because we were there last year for a rabbit hunt." They have a big running of hares each year at Drumlanrig, and give the game to the villagers to make hare soup. That's a custom something like corned beef and cabbage on St. Patrick's Day here in the United States.

I asked them, "Who did you see up there at Drumlanrig?"

"Oh, Johnny Dalkieth was there," Ludavic said. "We were together at Oxford, and that's what we called him—Johnny. We know Drumlanrig very well."

Later, toward the fall—I remember it was the time of the year when the sandhill cranes were flying south—I was at my desk writing one day, and Evelyn came in and said, "There's a young man here from Scotland. He'd like to meet you." So I left my desk and went out. There were two men standing there. One was a man from the forest service whose name was Kirkpatrick, which is a Scottish name. The other fellow was a younger man. After I shook hands with both of them, I said to the younger one, "I understand you're from Scotland."

He said, "Yes, I am. I thought I'd drop by here."

I said, "Well, I came to New Mexico from Scotland."

He nodded his head and asked, "Where were you in Scotland?" When I said, "Drumlanrig," he started grinning, and he said, "Well, isn't that a coincidence! Drumlanrig Castle is my house."

I looked at him then, and I said, "You're Johnny Dalkieth." He stood there laughing and admitted, "Yes, I am."

I said, "Ludavic Kennedy was here awhile ago."

"Yes," he said, "they told me about you, so I wanted to stop by and see you." He was interested in forestry; the forest service man was showing him around, and was taking him up to the Jemez Mountains so he could see the logging that was going on up there.

We talked for a while, and then the two men left and went up to the Jemez, and Evelyn and I started walking to Bernalillo to do our shopping. As we were on our way back, we stopped at the side of the road, where there was a sandhill crane that had been wounded. We didn't know what to do with it. The road was just down below us, and we heard a horn toot, and here was Johnny Dalkieth waving at us; he was going back to town. He gave us a lift to the monument, and we kept the crane there a couple of days until someone from the zoo came out and got it.

Rebecca West came through, too. She was one of the famous writers of Britain at that time and, of course, a great friend, and lover, of H. G. Wells—in fact, Anthony West is the son of H. G. Wells and Rebecca West. She was visiting Miss Bieber in Santa Fe, and Miss Bieber was showing her around. It was the day of the San Felipe Dance at San Felipe Pueblo, so Miss Bieber had decided that she'd take Rebecca to San Felipe and then over to the monument and have me explain Indian life to her. I took her into the kiva and showed her around, and then she came into the house and we talked. Her husband was with her, too.

As I was taking her to the kiva, an old dog came over to us. It was originally Jimmy Barela's dog from Santa Ana, but he had waded the river and come over to the monument and made his home there. We sort of adopted him. He was a black dog with a growth of red hair all over the front of his face. Rebecca West had just been to San Felipe, and she had seen the Koshares—the clowns—and their faces looked the same as the dog's. She looked down at the dog, and she said, "Oh, look at that dog. What's his name?"

I said, "Well, he doesn't have a name. We just call him 'old dog.'"

She said, "Well, from now on he has a name. I am calling him Koshare."

Pueblo Indian Friends

In 1948, the year after Evelyn and I married, the museum took us away from the monument and sent us to Chicago to the Railroad Fair, where all the railroads in the United States had their famous trains on exhibit—the Super Chief, the Hiawatha, the Twentieth Century Limited, and the Broadway Limited—all the great trains. That was the height of the railroad era, and it was a very successful exhibition.

The Santa Fe Railroad, of course, wanted to exploit the Indians. They had so many Indians there—Zunis, Navajos, Kiowas, Apaches—and the Rio Grande Pueblos. The Santa Anas were there, too; and that's why we were there.

Edmund Ladd was in charge of the Indians and the pueblo at the fair. They had built a big pueblo—not of adobe, but it looked exactly like an Indian pueblo in New Mexico, with ladders going up on to terraces. That's where the Indians stayed.

Then there was a long building with a walk in the middle of it and, on both sides, a platform where the Indians would be making pottery or carving kachina dolls. A Navajo woman would be at her loom weaving a blanket, a Hopi man would be at his loom. Someone from Santa Ana would sit there carving the little wooden burros that he was famous for. All the Indian crafts of New Mexico were done there, and the tourists would walk through the building looking at the Indians. Evelyn and I had a desk at the end of the building where the tourists were supposed to come and ask questions about what the Indians were doing. Some of the questions were terrific, and some of them were not. I remember one incident in particular. I was sitting at my desk, and a woman came walking by with two little kids. She was making her way out, and one of the little kids said, "I wanna see the Indians!" She said, "Oh, they're not Indians. They're just dressed up as Indians. There are no Indians anymore. The U.S. Cavalry killed 'em all off."

Photos from the Chicago Railroad Fair, 1948. Above, a Navajo sandpainting. Below and opposite: Friends from Santa Ana Pueblo and elsewhere.

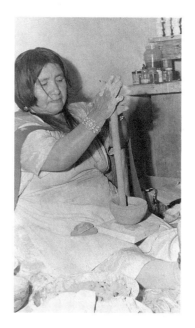

115

*Mural in the Painted Kiva at the Coronado State Monument.
Figures found during the 1930s' excavations were restored and
reproduced for exhibits.*

Things like that went on all the time there.

It was the same thing at the Coronado State Monument. People
would come in and ask the most ridiculous questions. One time I was
taking some tourists around the monument, and they were terribly
interested in everything. I took them to the ruins, and then we went
down into the kiva, and I was explaining some things to them. All of a
sudden we looked up, and down through the hatchway came a couple
of Santo Domingo Indians. The Indians were going around looking at
the figures on the wall and talking in their language. Then the hatchway filled up again with a group of people, and a woman came

*Evelyn and John Sinclair on their patio, with friends
from Santa Ana Pueblo.*

down. Somebody asked, "What's down there?" The woman said, "Why, nothing. No need to come down." The Indians just stood there, and one of them finally said, "These pictures around here—they are everything that we believe. They show us how to live. To us, these paintings are everything to live for. But that woman who just left here—she doesn't like classical music; she just likes cowboy music."

I've always remembered that.

Evelyn always had great respect for the Indians. She fit right in with them, and they just loved her. When she was at the anthropology laboratory in Santa Fe, she would come down to Zia Pueblo, and at one time she spent six weeks with a friend who taught at the school there. So she knew a lot of the Zias before we were married. She didn't know the Santa Anas then, but they were both very close to us in our early married life. At the monument, Indian friends from both Santa Ana and Zia pueblos would come to visit us—and particularly Evelyn. They were just crazy about her, and they called her Eveleen. Our house was always full of Indians.

Evelyn took on a few little projects of her own while at the monument, such as trying to get the Santa Anas back to arts and crafts again. She encouraged a lot of the Santa Ana women to make pottery.

The monument was right on the bank of the Rio Grande, and the pueblo was on the other bank, a mile or so beyond. There was a special clay by the monument that the Spaniards called *desquila*. It was found where at one time they had the dipping vats for sheep around Bernalillo. Right at that place, there was a deposit of clay that had a lot of oil in it, and for many years, the Zias had come down to get that clay from this little pocket. Evelyn knew that this clay was ideal for ceramics, and so, with her one hand, she would fill a bucket with that clay and wade across the river, carrying it over to Santa Ana Pueblo, where she would try to instruct Indians in making pottery.

One woman, Crisinciana Peña, the wife of the *cacique*, or religious leader, had already been making pottery, but only to a limited extent. Evelyn took her in hand and rekindled her interest in pottery-making. She was very, very old. Then Crisinciana's daughter; her sister, Dora Montoya; and several other women also became interested.

Of course, the inevitable happened. After a while, the Indians really got into it, and then somebody from the university in Albuquerque stepped in and, out of the clear blue sky, took over the project. Evelyn and all her good work were forgotten. That other person got the credit.

Evelyn was an artist in her own right. There on the wall are some of the paintings she did at the monument. She had a studio in the entrance house there, and she was inspired by the mountains. Rex Arrowsmith of the Fenn Galleries in Santa Fe came down and visited with me a few years ago in our house in Bernalillo, in 1970 or thereabouts. Evelyn at that time was teaching school in Acomita at Acoma Pueblo. Rex had bought a few Indian things from us, and he came in and looked at a painting that Evelyn had done of the Sandia Mountains. This man from the Fenn Galleries looked at that painting and asked, "Who painted that?"

I said, "Evelyn, my wife."

He looked at it again and asked, "Why? . . .why would anybody who can paint like that . . . What is she doing teaching school?"

I've told Evelyn that story many, many times, but she continued to

John Sinclair at work, circa 1952.

teach, and I'm glad she did. While we were at the monument, though, she did a lot of painting. We still have many of her pieces stacked in the corner over in back of the telephone table.

Evelyn painted and taught, and I wrote and took care of the monument. I always wanted to write about the beautiful country that I had come to, and the time had come that I could devote myself to it full-time.

Evelyn Fox Sinclair, 1975.
Pastel drawing by Ed DeLavy.

After Many a Harvest

I retired from Coronado State Monument on December 31, 1962, and on New Year's Day of 1963 I moved down to Rodeo, a little town located in the extreme southwest corner of New Mexico, about a mile or so from the Arizona border. Evelyn had been living and teaching in Rodeo since August 1962, and I went down there to gather material for *Cowboy Riding Country*. Rodeo was a nice little place in a desert valley that sloped up into the Chiricahua Mountains, which were very beautiful. We stayed in Rodeo about two and one-half years, and then moved to Columbus, the site of Pancho Villa's raid, right on the Mexican border, where Evelyn taught school to children not only from Columbus but also from Palomas on the Mexican side. I had bought a few acres of land there, but we weren't there long before we both became homesick for northern New Mexico. Evelyn then found a teaching job in Placitas, a community on the western slope of the Sandia Mountains, not far from the monument. So we moved to Placitas, and Evelyn taught there for three years.

In 1968 Evelyn took a job with the Bureau of Indian Affairs, and taught school at Acomita, one of the Acoma Pueblo villages. She would spend the week at Acomita and the weekends at our new home here. We had just moved to this house on the reservation. I fixed the place up, and I did a lot of writing while she was teaching school. When Evelyn retired from teaching, she occupied herself going to the University of New Mexico in Albuquerque, taking courses, studying art and painting a little; and she also helped me out by doing some research.

We settled here at Santa Ana to be close to the river, to the monument, to our friends; and we've stayed here because we got on with the Indians quite well.

This was Indian cattle country, and the grass is still good. When I was at the Coronado State Monument, the Santa Ana Pueblo range rider lived here, and we were friends.

The author, 1975.

The house was built in 1938 by Sophie Aberle, who was the head of the Indian Service in Albuquerque at that time. The stones that are in the walls, and the flagstones on the floor here, were brought over all the way from Acoma, and the vigas were hauled down from the Jemez Mountains. Santa Ana Indians built it for her under the direction of an Italian construction boss who was an expert mason.

Sophie Aberle built the house as a retreat, but after she married, she didn't come out here so much, and Bureau of Indian Affairs people came out here to have parties. The road out front wasn't there at that time; there was just a two-rut dirt road that came up by the Coronado State Monument. And there was nothing around here—nothing but this house and Mrs. Duke's homestead, which was down where the

Prairie Star Restaurant is now on the highway. Then after the BIA got tired of coming out here, the Indians took it over, and they started renting it out.

It was through me that the Indians got a couple of university students who wanted to live here. They fixed it up, and the Indians rented it out for five dollars a month. All they had here was water; there was no electricity, no telephone. But they had water in the tank outside, and it came down to a faucet. There was a sink in here too, but that's all there was—a sink and a faucet. Later there was a couple of other university students. They had the electricity put in here because, by that time, there was an electric line to the Jemez Dam, and they hooked onto that. Then the new paved road was put in.

I brought the first propane in. Before that there was just an oil heater, and before that only a fireplace that heated the house.

When I rented it in 1967, the Indians raised the rent to ten dollars a month. Afterward, every time the lease was renewed, they put it up a little bit. Then it was fifteen dollars; then fifty dollars; and now it's a hundred dollars a month.

This is our home—not in Bernalillo, because I didn't want to live in a town, surrounded by people—but here on the old range. Writing is a very lonely job—solitary and sedentary. You've got to be in one place all the time. It takes a long time to think about things. That's why I like it here.

I follow Thoreau's views on life thoroughly. All of his sayings appeal to me. He wrote, "I had rather sit on a pumpkin and have it all to myself than to be crowded on a velvet cushion." That's what I want to do—and the most amazing thing is that I've always lived this Thoreauvian life and didn't know it until pretty late in life.

Thoreau said that he could support himself by working six weeks of the year. I did the same thing. I rented a cabin on the north side of the Capitans and lived in that cabin by myself. I had time to think. I had time to study nature—the mountains and the wildlife around me—and I had no idea that I was living Thoreau's way of life.

It was in 1943 that I discovered Thoreau. I had just come back from Tucson and had set up shop in Santa Fe, but I wanted to spend Lent—and especially Holy Week—with the Penitentes of northern New

Mexico so that I could study them. I rented a little studio outside the village of Alcalde, which is above Española, north of San Juan Pueblo. The studio, surrounded by green fields, was owned by Dorothy Kent, the sister of Rockwell Kent, the famous painter and illustrator. The whole area was Spanish, Penitente mostly, and I studied their ways as much as I possibly could by talking to people around there and by doing a considerable amount of reading. Of course, a lot of people had written about the Penitentes before—Alice Corbin Henderson, in particular—but I wanted to get my information firsthand. And I did; my next book will have an article drawing on my research from that time.

I paid ten dollars a month rent for my studio, and I was supposed to milk Dorothy's two cows, feed the chickens, and plant a garden. That spring I planted one acre in garden—tomatoes, eggplant, chile, bell peppers, and yellow corn—and I was very good at that because of what I had learned in Scotland.

That was the way I lived that spring. I had no money at all. I hadn't written anything for *New Mexico Magazine* recently, and I wasn't working for the museum anymore. So Dorothy asked me one day, "Have you ever read Thoreau?"

I said, "No, I haven't. Tell me about him."

She said, "Thoreau lived like you do."

I had told her about working on the cattle ranches and about living off by myself and not really caring about money or a car. But everybody I knew down there had wanted something. Back in the Capitans, twice a year by mail car the catalogs would come in from Sears, Roebuck, and Montgomery Ward, and Bellas Hess; and all the people along the route would devour those catalogs. And what they wanted! But there was nothing in them that I wanted, or that I really needed. I didn't have a car, but I had three horses, and they were sufficient to get me around.

Dorothy told me, "You live just like Thoreau did. That was his doctrine, his philosophy." And she said, "I'm going to give you a copy of *Walden Pond*."

So she went to Santa Fe and brought me back a copy of *Walden Pond*. That paperback is now just absolutely worn to pieces. The pages are falling out because I've read it so much—over and over and over again. Everything that Thoreau preached—and he wasn't a preacher, mind you; he never went to church—I was doing. "A man is rich in proportion to the number of things he can afford to leave alone," he wrote. I could leave a terrible lot alone—all those things in the Montgomery Ward catalog that everybody called the "Wish Book" because they wished for this, and they wished for that.

I didn't. I would go to town on horseback to buy my groceries and whatever else I needed, and I was always well fed. I would work only about half the year, and I had plenty. I would go down to Picacho and work on the sheep ranches when spring came; when the lambing came on, I would get about six weeks work down there. Then in the summertime the shearing would come on; and in the fall, we'd drive the flocks down to Roswell to the stockyard. On the cattle ranches in spring, there would be the cattle roundup and branding, and also a horse roundup. Then in the fall, there would be the shipping of the cattle—driving them down to the Riverside Stockyards in Roswell. Between these jobs, I had all this time to myself—to read, to think, to ride around, to go up onto the summit of the Capitan Mountains for a few days and camp out. . . .

In a way, Thoreau's love for simplicity influenced my later writing because simplicity became my style. When I wrote *In Time of Harvest*, what influenced me were those homesteaders that I had met and studied, and who were my friends when I was up on the north side of the Capitan Mountains—people who drove wagons, rode go-devils, and grew crops of pinto beans.

Instead of thrashing the bean crop in the thrashing machine, they'd thrash it in a wagon. Somebody'd throw the bean plants up on the wagon, and another would pound them with a pitchfork and then throw the hay off to one side. Then they would throw more plants on the wagon and pound them; and after a while the wagon would get half-full with pinto beans. That was the simplicity that I admire.

Before I wrote *In Time of Harvest*, I never thought anything about my style except that I knew if I wanted to write articles as I had been doing, I would have to write short sentences and pack as many facts into a paragraph as I possibly could.

Back in Tucson, where I had completed the first draft of *In Time of Harvest*, Harold Latham of the Macmillan Company met me on the platform of the railroad station with the manuscript of the book. He had done some editing on it while on a trip all the way from New York to San Francisco. Then in Tucson he had the manuscript ready for me to revise. He wanted me to put another chapter in it to add some drama near the end of the novel—that and some other changes. Harold Latham, one of the greatest authorities on literature in America—if it weren't for Latham, Margaret Mitchell's *Gone with the Wind* might never have been published—he told me there, "John, your style in *In Time of Harvest* is not that of an article writer." He said, "You have a certain style that has a lyric to it. When you read your writing of the language of these people," he said, "you're reading a form of poetry." *The Chicago Tribune*, in its review of the book, said that John L. Sinclair writes "like mountain music turned prose and put between bean rows."

So, from then on I had an entirely different style of writing. It wasn't that cramped paragraph where everything is jammed together and you try to get the article over with. I began to give myself leeway. Latham had said, "Never, never write in any other form. That's your style of writing. All your books from now on—write them in that style." *Death in the Claimshack* and *Cousin Drewey and the Holy Twister* are in that style. But that damned me for writing anything for the American mainstream; I can't write for them anymore. But the people of the Southwest—they can understand what I write.

Besides Thoreau, very few writers had any influence on me. Maybe Erskine Caldwell did because he had written *Tobacco Road* about that same time, and perhaps Roark Bradford, Richard Bradford's father, whose *John Henry* and other works used Negro dialect, while I used the vernacular of the homesteaders from Arkansas and Oklahoma. I think they were my main influence—those people I knew in the Capitan Mountains.

The homesteaders were of the earth. The cowboy was not earthy. The cowboy was in the business of raising beef, and he put a lot of acrobatics into it. I believe the cattle industry could have survived without all that rough stuff, so the cowboy didn't impress me much. It was the earthiness of the wagon people that impressed me, and that was also what I liked about Thoreau.

I'm still writing nearly every day, but I write less now than I did a few years ago. I felt much younger then. I used to get up in the middle of the night, sit down at my desk, and write on the typewriter for a couple of hours—sometimes until three or four in the morning. I would really put out the stuff. But now it's not like that.

Age is part of it. When you're ninety, you slow down some. A few years ago, when I broke my hip and was laid up in a nursing home, I didn't do any writing at all for a while. I'm better now, and have a few more stories to tell.

I try to keep in touch with other writers. Elmer Kelton and I write to each other. He has a downtown office in San Angelo, Texas, and is connected with the Cattlemen's Association there. He writes a lot for the cattlemen and for Texas magazines, and has written several fine books. Among them are *The Day the Cowboys Quit* and *The Year It Never Rained*. Nelson Nye, my old shoot-'em-up-bang-bang writer friend, lives in Tucson, and we talk on the phone now and then. He writes just as it says on his letterhead—"Manufacturer of Blood and Thunder." Frank Waters and I talk on the telephone nearly every week; we're the same age.

Some have called me the dean of New Mexican authors, but I certainly am not. A deputy dean, maybe, but there are many other deputies, and they are all ahead of me. Frank Waters is the dean of southwestern writers; he's been at it a long time.

Hal Rhodes of KNME-TV in Albuquerque interviewed me several years ago, and asked me the question, "Did it ever dawn on you, while you were in Scotland, that you would one day become a member of the Cowboy Hall of Fame?" My answer, of course, was that I could not have imagined that—but my writing has resulted in some awards coming my way. There were three awards in one year alone. There was the Cowboy Hall of Fame's Western Heritage Wrangler Award, the Western Writers' Golden Spur Award, and then the Western Heritage Center's Honorary Life Membership in the Cowboy Hall of Fame, all in 1978. In 1986 there was a second Western Heritage Wrangler Award, and then last year, a few days after my ninetieth birthday, Bruce King, the governor of New Mexico, gave me the Governor's Award for Excellence and Achievement in the Arts.

Most of the awards were awards for articles in *New Mexico Magazine*. The 1978 Wrangler and Spur awards were for an article that came out in 1977 titled "Where the Cowboys Hunkered Down." It later became the first chapter in *Cowboy Riding Country*. The 1986 Wrangler Award was for "Santa Rita del Cobre," a story on the Santa Rita copper pit down near Silver City. In all, I've written over thirty-five articles for *New Mexico Magazine*; my latest, "The Hasty Career of the Copycat Kid," is in the February 1993 issue.

The honor that means the most to me is the one hanging up over my desk, the Honorary Life Membership in the Cowboy Hall of Fame. The others are quite prestigious, of course, but they don't give those life memberships to you every year.

Looking back over my life, I have very few regrets, and if I had it all to do over again, I don't think I'd have done it any differently. Maybe I could have gone on to British Columbia and started a fruit farm in the Okanagan Valley; and maybe I could have had a cattle ranch up on the Fraser River, and made frequent trips to Scotland. That is what I was expected to do, but I don't regret not having done that.

I'm perfectly satisfied with what I've accomplished. For although it's true that I've had a lonely life, I've never been lonely in my life. Solitude is my favorite state.

What is it that Thoreau said about solitude? That the good life is simplicity, independence, magnanimity, and solitude.

He was describing my life.